A Survival Guide for Selling a Home

A Survival Guide for Selling a Home

Sid Davis

AMACOM

American Management Association

New York • Atlanta • Brussels • Chicago • Mexico City • San Francisco
Shanghai • Tokyo • Toronto • Washington, D.C.

*Special discounts on bulk quantities of AMACOM books are
available to corporations, professional associations, and other
organizations. For details, contact Special Sales Department,
AMACOM, a division of American Management Association,
1601 Broadway, New York, NY 10019.*
Tel.: 212-903-8316. Fax: 212-903-8083.
Web site: www.amacombooks.org

*This publication is designed to provide accurate and authoritative
information in regard to the subject matter covered. It is sold with
the understanding that the publisher is not engaged in rendering
legal, accounting, or other professional service. If legal advice or other
expert assistance is required, the services of a competent professional
person should be sought.*

*REALTOR® is a registered collective membership mark that
identifies a real estate professional who is a member of the National
Association of REALTORS® and subscribes to its strict Code of
Ethics. AMACOM uses this term throughout this book in initial
capital letters or ALL CAPITAL letters for editorial purposes only,
with no intention of trademark violation.*

Library of Congress Cataloging-in-Publication Data

Davis, Sid
    A survival guide to selling a home / Sid Davis.
       p. cm.
    Includes index.
    ISBN 0-8144-7274-5
    1. House selling—United States.   2. Residential real estate—United States.
    I. Title.

    HD259.D385   2005
    643'.12—dc22   2004021064

Printing Number

10 9 8 7 6 5 4 3 2 1

Contents

Preface

For most of us buying a home is not only the biggest investment of our lives, but it's also one of the longest running financial commitments. For thirty years this commitment typically claims from 25 percent to 50 percent of a homeowner's monthly income to pay the principal, interest, taxes, insurance, and upkeep. Few other investments demand more or can be as profitable and satisfying as home ownership.

Yet, it's amazing how casual so many homeowners are about their investment. No way would they tolerate a loss on their 401(k) or even on selling a car the way many do on selling their homes. Many times I've seen homeowners spend much time and effort detailing a vehicle they plan to sell, just so they can get a few hundred dollars more. Yet when it comes time to sell their home, they plant a *For Sale* sign in the lawn and consider the prep work done. They're oblivious to the reality that this approach can cost them thousands of dollars, and sometimes even enough money to buy a new car or two!

Over the years I've come to the realization that this casual home selling attitude is due to three things:

1. Unlike detailing a car, where most owners intuitively know what to do, getting a home ready to market is on a par with quantum mechanics: It's neither intuitive nor obvious.

2. The thought of getting the home into top shape for selling is intimidating to many because they don't have a clue where to start or what to do.

3. Owners don't want to admit they're clueless and hope that if they put up a sign eventually the tooth fairy will smile on their

effort and a buyer will come along. They don't realize that time is not on their side: The mortgage-interest clock keeps ticking, and the longer a home is on the market the less it sells for.

Fortunately, I've also found that with a little coaching and a clear game plan to follow, most home sellers can sell their homes faster and for more money.

Whether you're working with a Realtor or selling a home yourself, the following chapters will show you what to do and what mistakes to avoid. This book will give you a roadmap to follow, from prepping your home to depositing the biggest closing check possible. When you follow the tips and suggestions, your home will sell quickly, even in a slow market.

In these pages you'll learn:

- How to put your home in selling condition so it outshines the competition

- How to know which improvements pay off and which ones just cost you money

- How to showcase your home so buyers will choose your home over others for sale in your area

- Pricing techniques that will ensure you sell your home for the highest price possible

- How to market your home and attract buyers who pay top dollar

- How to work with buyers in both hot and cold markets

- How to find a good agent and get the best deal

When you sell, you'll probably need to buy another home, so there's a chapter on how to find your next home and get the best deal. Also included is a chapter on holding garage sales and how to pick and get the best deal on movers.

All told, this book will save you lots of time and thousands of dollars using little known tricks of the trade I have used in buying and selling my own investment properties. Whether you use an agent or act on your own, this book shows the right path, clearly marked, so the process becomes fun rather than a stressful have-to project.

To this end, many thanks are due to all the homeowners I've

worked with over the years, whose selling experiences, mistakes, and happy endings have made this book possible. I especially appreciate those home sellers who generously agreed to let me use their mistakes and experiences in the examples, so that others may profit from them.

Selling FSBO or Using an Agent

When the time comes to sell, many sellers go through the migraine-generating process of deciding whether to sell on their own or find an agent. It can take several days mentally batting back and forth the pros and cons before a decision is reached.

Home-selling factors and conditions are constantly changing, and sometimes you have to change that decision. For example, you may start out going FSBO (for sale by owner) and find you're not getting buyers through your home for some reason. If so, something has to change, and you have to be flexible enough to recognize that. If you want to move anytime soon, you may have to rethink your options and consider the *multiple listing service,* or MLS, run by Realtors. And yes, you'll have to give up some equity to pay Realtor fees.

With that in mind, this chapter will go through the pros and cons of selling on your own versus listing with an agent. Other important topics covered are how to find an agent, all about buyer and seller agency, and what to do if your agent isn't getting your house sold. But first, here are some reasons why selling your home yourself can be a good idea.

The Case for Selling FSBO

Of course, by far the biggest reason most homeowners have for wanting to sell on their own is saving a big chunk of equity, money that can cover the closing costs or down payment on your next home.

For example, a 6 percent fee on a $225,000 home is $13,500. That can be a huge incentive to try selling by owner, especially when:

1. *It's a hot market.* Homes are selling fast, multiple offers are common, and all the promotion you need is from a yard sign or word-of-mouth.

In one instance, Rhonda told a coworker in her law office that she was going to sell her home. The coworker, familiar with the house, thought she and her husband could qualify and made an appointment to come over that night and write up an offer.

2. *You have a buyer lined up.* A neighbor or someone you know wants to buy your home. This often happens when your home is in great condition and in a super location. Everyone who sees it becomes a sales person for you.

This is borne out by National Association of Realtors' figures that report about 14 percent of home sellers sold their own home in 2003, and of those buyers, 44 percent knew the seller.

3. *You're in a great neighborhood that has few homes for sale, and those that do go on the market sell fast for a premium.* People cruise these neighborhoods looking for *For Sale* signs to pop up. It can be like throwing your baited hook into a pond of starving fish when you plant that sign.

4. *You haven't been in the home for long and don't have any equity.* In other words, you're selling the home for what you owe, and any fees would have to come out of your pocket.

5. *You're building a new home or have several months to experiment before the pressure to sell kicks in.* Some home sellers get tripped up on this one. They put their home up for sale and when it sells the next day they have nowhere to go. It becomes a scramble to find a short-term rental, and they end up moving twice.

The message here is to line up your ducks before you plant the sign.

The Case for Listing with an Agent

How you look at this situation can get controversial. Agents say buyers try to take advantage of FSBOs by making low offers, knowing the sellers don't have professional help to advise them. On the other side of the argument, FSBO advocates say these price reductions usually don't equal what a seller would pay out in commissions.

Though far from a scientific study, anecdotal data and personal experience over the past two decades would suggest that in a normal to slow market, FSBOs usually end up selling for 5 to 10 percent less than asking price.

In a sizzling market, who knows. Homes sell so fast that buyers wonder if they could have gotten more if they would have asked. But, it's certain that without access to daily MLS sold data, you'll leave money on the table.

You'll probably want to list your home with a Realtor if:

- You have to sell fast and need all the heavyweight marketing you can get from the MLS and an agent's contacts

- It's a slow market and homes need extra exposure and an agent's savvy to attract buyers.

- You don't feel comfortable dealing with buyers or negotiating offers on your own.

- You don't have the time or want to deal with the sales process. For example, one couple said they didn't want anything to do with selling their home. They wanted to insulate themselves completely from showing the home or meeting potential buyers. They just couldn't stand the thought of people going through their home and bad-mouthing their decorating.

- You have no way to screen unqualified buyers or tire kickers who waste your time. A parade of unqualified lookers going through your home can get old fast.

- You're uncomfortable letting strangers walk through your home and want the security of an agent screening them first and being there for showings.

- Because of your work schedule, you have difficulty showing your home.

- Your mother-in-law is an agent. This is a sticky one—good luck!

Before you list with an agent, you'll want to know the rules of the game on who represents whom. The next section on agency tells all.

All About Buyer and Seller Agency

Until recently, when you bought a home through a Realtor you probably assumed the agent was representing you in the transaction. [Note: In this book, Realtor refers to an agent who belongs to the National Association of Realtors and subscribes to their Code of Ethics. Only Realtors have access to the MLS.] In reality, the agent most likely represented and had a fiduciary duty to the sellers. If your agent found you a home through the multiple listing system and cooperated with the listing office, your agent was still working for the sellers as a sub-agent. As a buyer you were not represented and were on your own.

Home sellers also were exposed to additional liability because traditionally the agents in the MLS represented the sellers as sub-agents, and a lawsuit resulting from agent misrepresentation usually ended up embroiling the homeowner as well.

To correct this imbalance, state legislators over the past several years have created three broad classes of agency representation: seller's agency, buyer's agency, and dual or limited agency. However, a fourth class, called facilitator status, is starting to gain momentum in some states where the real estate agent represents neither buyer nor seller.

Seller Agency: The Agent Represents the Homeowner

When you list your home with a Realtor you create a seller-agency relationship. Your agent represents you and your interests in finding a buyer with the price and terms you specify in the listing agreement.

If your home is placed on a MLS, you have the choice of offering sub-agency and letting cooperating agents from other brokerages become your sub-agents, or you can cooperate with buyer agents only and not offer sub-agency. Sub-agency is fast disappearing because of the liability you may incur when all agents on an MLS can represent you. Some areas still have this option on the listing agreement; if the form you're using has that check box, make sure you don't check or initial it.

Listing or seller agency forms vary from state to state and even sometimes by county, but the basics are these:

- An agent representing a home seller must have a written agency agreement defining the scope of the agency, and must disclose that agency to a prospective buyer.

- A seller's agent acts solely on behalf of the sellers and has a fiduciary obligation to them in selling their home.

■ The agent is obligated to disclose to the seller all material information the agent learns about the buyer or about the sales transaction. For example, suppose your home is listed for $175,000 and an offer comes in from another agent for $165,000. If your agent finds out the buyer is qualified for the full sales price or is willing to pay more, it's her duty to inform you. Otherwise, you may be influenced to accept a low offer.

■ The listing agent should not disclose any information that will weaken the seller's bargaining position or adversely affect the sale.

In other words, your agent should watch what they say to a buyer's agent who calls about your house. Sometimes an agent will blurt out information that can affect your bottom line, for example, by answering questions such as:

"Will they take less if we make an offer?"
"What's the seller's bottom line?"
"What's their loan balance?"
"Are they behind in their mortgage payments?"
"How soon do they have to move?"

You get the idea.

In one case, a buyer's agent presented an offer to the sellers and their agent that was $7,000 under the listing price. Unfortunately, the offer had attached to it a letter from the lender stating the buyers were qualified for the full listing price. This resulted in the sellers countering back for a few thousand dollars more.

The sellers would have accepted the offer as written, but when they read that the buyers qualified for more they decided to counter. The buyer's agent should have asked the lender in their letter to simply confirm the buyers were prequalified for the offer amount.

The seller's agent did her job by pointing out what the buyers qualified for and suggesting they counter. But, the buyer's agent cost his clients a few thousand dollars by missing what the prequalifying letter said or by not realizing its significance to the deal.

Because of agents (and homeowners too) talking too much, the old World War II poster, "Loose lips sink ships," should be reworded to "Loose lips cost clients money" and posted in real estate offices.

It's important to note that agency agreements don't require agents to—nor should they—lie about defects in the property or the seller's ability to perform their obligations. Common examples are the sellers' inability to convey clear title, or property defects the sellers know about but try to hide.

Buyer's Agents Represent the Buyer Only

As mentioned earlier, when buyers contact an agent to find their dream home, they most likely will sign a buyer representation agreement where the agent agrees to represent them.

Since you've committed to pay a brokerage fee to the listing broker only, it's his responsibility to split the fee with the selling office or buyer's broker. This commission split is disclosed on the listing form. In some areas it is split 50:50, but it can be whatever the brokers on the MLS agree on in your area.

Buyer's agency forms vary from state to state but the basics are similar:

- An agent representing a buyer must have a written agency agreement defining the scope of the agency.

- A Buyer's agent acts solely on behalf of the buyer and owes the buyer his/her loyalty.

- All information between agent and buyer that would weaken the buyer's bargaining position is to be kept confidential.

- The buyer's broker is responsible for all earnest-money deposits.

- The broker should disclose to sellers and other agents when they make an offer that they are representing the buyers and have a signed agency agreement.

A Note of Caution on Commission Splits

If the usual commission split in your area is 3 percent to the buyer's broker you don't want to show anything less on the listing agreement. If you offered 2 percent, for example, your home may not get shown once other agents see the commission split is lower on your home than on other listings in your area.

In other words, make sure that when an agent makes you a deal on the commission, she is not shorting the buyer's agent split that is common in your area.

Of course, this agency agreement does not permit the agent to misrepresent the buyer's financial condition or ability to perform when presenting an offer.

What About an Agent Representing Both Buyer and Seller?

If you happen to drop in an open house and find it's your dream home and that unless you move quickly you'll lose it, can the listing agent work with you and write up the offer? With few exceptions, yes.

When a Realtor represents both buyer and seller this is called dual or limited agency. There is some controversy with dual agency, and some brokers feel the potential liability is great enough to avoid it.

However, most brokers will represent buyers and sellers in a sale with both sides signing a disclosure form, and both sides are usually happy with the results.

Most problems associated with dual agency have been the agents' failure to properly disclose they were working for both parties. State real estate regulators consider it a cardinal sin if you fail to disclose who an agent is working for.

As with other agency agreements, dual or limited agency paperwork will vary from state to state. However, the common framework is:

1. An agent who represents both buyer and seller must have a written agreement with both parties consenting to and defining the scope of the limited agency.

2. Because agents who act for both buyer and seller are in a contradictory position, they must be neutral and cannot disclose any information that will harm either side's bargaining position.

Sometimes having an experienced agent represent both parties can be a huge plus in putting the deal together. The agent knows what needs to be done to make the transaction work and can guide both parties to a win-win sale.

What If You Want to Sell and Then Buy Another Home with the Same Agent?

This is usually not a problem because the seller's agency in force for the sale of your home ends at closing. Buying another home creates a new agency relationship when you sign the buyer's representation form and go house hunting even if your old home hasn't closed yet.

Leon and Alyssa did this when they sold their 1950s bungalow and moved up to a newer two-story home. They were so happy with the way their listing agent handled their sale that they wouldn't consider using anyone else.

The day they signed an offer on their bungalow they also signed a buyer's agency and started looking for a new home. Within a week they found exactly what they were looking for and made an offer subject to the sale on their home closing.

Using the same agent for both selling their old home and finding a new one worked out great. Their agent was able to coordinate the transactions so Leon and Alyssa were able to close back-to-back and could move from the old home right into the new one.

Transaction-Broker or Facilitator May Be the Future

Different from the buyer's and seller's agencies discussed, an emerging concept called transaction-brokerage is gaining momentum across the country. A transaction-broker works with the consumer without establishing an agency relationship. The agent in effect becomes a facilitator working with a buyer or seller to put the deal together. Hopefully, the facilitator option will limit liability for the agent and the seller as well as give consumers a choice of how or whether they want to be represented.

Several states are considering this option, but so far Colorado is the only state that has passed legislation creating transaction-broker status. According to Colorado law, a broker is presumed to be a facilitator until the broker and consumer agree in writing to enter into a traditional agency relationship. However, the National Association of Realtors does not yet support the pure non-agency facilitator concept.

From the consumer's point of view, putting the agents under the spotlight to disclose whom they represent is a plus. It discourages misrepresentation and allows a home buyer to legally tap into the expertise of the agent. Ultimately that could translate into a smoother transaction for both buyer and seller.

Figure 1-1 summarizes the advantages and disadvantages of agencies.

How to Find a Good Agent

Realtors are professionals you hire to help you handle important events in your life, namely buying and selling a home. And as with mortgage lenders, home inspectors, and brain surgeons, you want the best. You want someone who can be objective, someone whose expertise you can tap into, someone who has the experience to get you out of any problems that are bound to come up without costing you big bucks.

FIGURE 1-1 Agency summary.	
Agency Options	**Advantages and Disadvantages**
Seller's Agency	When you list your home, you establish seller agency. You can limit that agency to the broker, or offer sub-agency to any or all agents on the MLS. However, you may be liable for the actions of agents from other brokerages when you offer sub-agency.
Buyer's Agency	When you, as a home buyer, contract with a Realtor to represent you, the agent has no duty or loyalty to the seller, and you have the advantage of his or her expertise and experience when making a buying decision. You can agree to exclusive or nonexclusive representation.
Dual or Limited Agency	A Realtor can represent both buyer and seller if both parties consent and agree in writing. The agent must remain neutral and say or do nothing that will harm either party's bargaining position. Because the potential for liability is high, some brokers and areas avoid this option.
Transaction Broker or Facilitator	The agent establishes no agency with either buyer or seller but works as a facilitator to put the deal together. This option is gaining popularity because it limits liability for both the agent and seller.

Go with a Professional, Not a Friend or Relative

One sunny weekend afternoon, Wes and Sheryl were driving through an area of new homes. One particular development caught their eye and they decided to check it out. The third model home they looked at was their dream home, with a perfect floor plan. They were so excited and felt life would have no meaning if they couldn't build a home just like it.

Going over the numbers with one of the builder's agents, Wes and Sheryl felt they had enough equity in their home to cover a 10 percent down payment plus closing costs. The agent told them they would have about 90 days to get their home sold and closed before the new home would be ready. The new homeowners-to-be eagerly signed the paperwork and gave the agent a $4,500 earnest-money check.

When they got home that evening, Sheryl called her aunt Wendy, who had just gotten her real estate license. Sheryl excitedly told her about the new home they were having built. She then asked Wendy to come over and list the home that evening.

Of course, Wendy was excited too, since this was her first listing and she wanted to show her niece and nephew what a good job she could do. She couldn't wait to take her office colleagues through the home on their weekly new listings tour as well as schedule an open house for that weekend.

Arriving at her appointment, Wendy chatted excitedly with Wes and Sheryl about their new home to be and how fast their home would sell. Wendy then pulled out her listing paperwork, and asked her new clients what they wanted to price their home at, her pen poised over the line labeled, "Listing Price."

The sellers looked at each other and then at Wendy. They weren't sure. Wes then suggested they take the mortgage balance, and add in what they needed to get into their next home along with the selling costs. It sounded good, so they added these up and wrote the total on the listing form.

On the following Wednesday, about a dozen agents from Wendy's office toured the home. Most of the agents did a quick walk-through, grabbed a brownie and bottle of Dasani water—compliments of the homeowner—and were out the door and on to the next home.

However, a couple of agents stayed for a moment and chatted with Wendy about her listing as they finished off the brownies. They expressed concern that the home was priced a little high for the neighborhood and asked her what comparables she used to come up with her price. This was Wendy's first inkling that maybe she had missed something vital.

Wendy did miss something vital. And long story short, the home didn't sell that month nor the next month nor the next. Agents showed it many times, but no one came through twice. The builder finished the house and sent Wes and Sheryl a final notice to close by the end of the month or they would lose their deposit and the home would go on the market.

But Lady Luck appeared to smile faintly when an offer came in a few days later. It was about 15 percent below asking price and the buyer wouldn't budge; it was a take-it-or-forget-it offer. The sellers were frantic and scheduled a meeting with Wendy's broker to see what they should do.

In the end, Wendy gave up her commission and her broker referred the sellers to a lender who put together a 100 percent financing package. Actually, it was more than 100 percent because the price was bumped up to cover some of the closing costs. The interest rate was a percent higher and the mortgage insurance (PMI) rate was $50 more a month. All total the house payment ended up $195 a month more than originally planned.

After the dust settled and with the clarity of 20/20 hindsight, what mistakes did Wes and Sheryl make?

1. They should never have committed to buying a new home until they had researched how saleable their current home was and have a backup plan in case the home didn't sell.

2. When relatives or close friends are involved, it's important to tread lightly. Your home is a big financial investment and listing your home with anyone for any reason other than their track record can come back to haunt you. In this case, they could have asked the broker to assign a top agent to co-list the home with Wendy.

Another option was to ask the broker or manager to go over the listing data and make sure it's realistic. In other words, be proactive and get backup from the real estate company when you're using a close friend or relative who is inexperienced.

3. They didn't do any homework on their own to determine the ballpark value of their home or how fast homes were selling in their area.

4. They should have talked with the broker after four or five qualified buyers had come through and showed no interest. In reality, agents were using the overpriced home to make the market-priced ones on their list look like better deals.

5. They made no effort to compare their home to the competition to see if improvements were needed to make it more saleable.

Obviously, a good Realtor could have prevented all this from happening. So how do you go about finding one?

Key to Finding a Professional
The best way to tell whether you're talking to a top agent or one blowing hot air is ask for MLS printouts of their last twelve sold listings. The printouts will show days on market (DOM), listed price, and sold price.

Interview, Then Decide

Finding a good Realtor is like finding a good lender: You need to talk to at least three prospects before you commit. If you know someone who bought a home recently and was happy with their agent, then add that agent to your short list.

Other good sources are mortgage lenders and title people. They know who the good agents are because they work with them on a daily basis and see how the deals are put together. After you've completed a short list of three or four agents, give them a call and chat about their expertise in your area and price range. If you eliminate one or two with your phone calls, that's fine. Set up an appointment with those you feel most comfortable with. Don't automatically assume the area superstar agent will be your best choice. She may be so busy that you end up working with an assistant most of the time.

An agent with a smaller or independent company who knows the area well and who has a good track record can be a good choice. How do you know if they have a good track record? Ask to see printouts of their last dozen sales.

Finally, make sure the agent you choose has a cell phone and is easy to contact; fast communication is important. With current technology there's no excuse for an agent not getting back to you within an hour or two of when you leave a message. If you get voice mail every time you call and she is slow to get back to you, seriously consider another agent.

Once you've found an agent with a good track record, the next important item is understanding the listing agreement.

The Listing Process

Three components of the listing process you'll be most concerned with are:

1. How long is the commitment time?

2. What is in the fine print?

3. What will it cost you?

If these are clearly understood and in writing, the process should go smoothly.

How Long Should You List?

Of course, most agents want as much time as they can get, but the norm for a commitment is three to six months, depending on the area and market. It also depends on how fast homes are selling in your market.

For instance, if the average days on market (DOM) in your price range and area is 36 days, then agreeing to a 45-to-60-day listing would be reasonable. But, if homes are taking five months to sell, then a six-month listing becomes reasonable.

Sometimes for unforeseen reasons a home doesn't sell within the DOM average. The home may be in good selling condition and buyers have come through, but there have been no offers. It can be one of those quirky things that's not your fault, your agent's fault, or even your house's fault.

Some common reasons for a slow sale are:

- Selling a home is a numbers game. You may have gotten a string of buyers who chose other homes for minor reasons like paint color, exterior color, the direction the home faces, etc.

- There may be a group of homes similar to yours that came on the market the same time you put your home up for sale. In this case it can take a month or two for the supply and demand to even out.

- When you put your home on the market, a national or local event dampened buying patterns for a while. These can be interest rate changes, bad economic indicators in the news, or a local employer announcing layoffs, and so on.

When this situation happens it's often better to extend the listing agreement rather than start over with a new agent and lose momentum.

Read the Fine Print

A good working relationship between you and your agent starts with everything in writing. Although each state has its own approved forms, the basics are similar. The checklist in Figure 1-2 gives you an idea of what you should focus on when a Realtor slides a listing form across the table for you to sign. The next section will tackle the sometimes controversial issue of real estate commissions and fees.

All About Commissions and Fees

Few topics invoke more emotion and controversy among home sellers than real estate commissions. Sellers want to keep as much equity as

FIGURE 1-2 Listing checklist.	
Item	**Explanation**
How Long Do You Sign Up For?	Average days-on-market of similar homes sold plus two weeks, or 45 days in a hot market.
Brokerage Fee	Make sure the percentage or fee is written in as you have agreed. A complete rundown of commission options are discussed in the next section.
Agent Protection Period	This protects the agent who shows the house. If a buyer to whom the agent has shown the house returns and wants to buy after the listing expires, you pay a commission. Go no more than one month on this line.
Cancellation Agreement	Few standard listing forms have this paragraph. You'll want to have the agent write in that if you're not happy you can cancel unconditionally. This becomes more important when listings go for two months or more.
Buyer's and Seller's Agency Explanations	Read over these paragraphs so you're familiar with who represents whom when an offer comes in.
Seller Authorizations	Check or initial the areas if you want the agent to have keys, put up signs, install lockboxes, etc. Make sure there are no authorizations to order title work, warranties, or other items that could cost you if the listing expires or a sale falls through.
Data Page or Attachment?	Make sure all the data about your house is accurate. You could be responsible if inaccurate data—such as age, square footage, or other facts—is advertised.
Who Should Sign a Listing Agreement?	Normally all parties who are listed on the title and have an interest in the property should sign the paperwork. To do otherwise can come back to haunt you.

possible, and agents want to get paid for their services. Is there a happy medium? It depends on whom you ask and how bad they want to sell their home. It also comes down to market conditions—selling in a sizzling market is much different from selling in a slow one. But, regardless of the market there are more listing and home-selling options than ever, and this next section will cover the more popular ones.

The Conventional Brokerage

The most common and high profile option is the usual exclusive agency listing. You list your home with a real estate brokerage and they take over for a commission of 5 to 7 percent of the sales price, collected at closing. Included in this package are advertising and listing on the MLS and Internet sites. It's a full-service package and works well for sellers who don't have the time or inclination to deal with the selling details.

Alonzo and Sandra went this route when they decided to retire and move to warmer climes. Wrapping up their retirement, they had little time to worry about house-selling details, so they started out by interviewing three agents actively selling in their neighborhood.

Although all the agents were professionals and had good track records selling homes in the area, Alonzo and Sandra chose the one with whom they felt most comfortable, and listed their home for $349,900.

The sign went on the lawn, images of the home's rooms and exterior were uploaded to the MLS Web site, and ads were run in the local weekly. Soon agents from other offices were bringing their clients through the house. This activity combined with the listing office's advertising brought over a dozen buyers through the house during the first week.

It wasn't long before the sellers accepted an offer and the paperwork headed for a closing. In reality, was the commission they paid to find a buyer worth it?

The sellers felt it was. They wanted a full-service package and were willing to pay 6 percent, or $20,700, to get their home sold. They had an agent that worked with them full time handling all the details and smoothing the way to closing. Did they have other options that would have cost less? Possibly, but it would have entailed them taking a more active role in the process. These sellers wanted to insulate themselves from the sales process so all they had to do was sign by the Xs when an acceptable offer came in.

On the other hand, if they wanted to do more than sign by the Xs and take on some of the marketing and sales responsibilities, they could have gone with brokers who offer discount packages. For a lower commission you can show your home yourself, and do the advertising or whatever you and the broker agree upon. How these programs work is next.

Discount Brokerages

Typical discount brokerages shave the commission from the traditional 6 or 7 percent to 5 or 4 percent. If the program offers to list your home on the MLS then you'll be subject to a 3 percent (or whatever's customary in your area) commission to the selling office. Usual discount broker options are listed in Figure 1-3.

Is the discount broker a good way to go? It all depends on how much of the sales process you want to get involved in and what the

FIGURE 1-3
Typical discount brokerage options.

Option	Your Cost
Fee Is a Percentage of Sales Price (MLS Participation)	Whatever the brokerage agrees to in addition to the 3 percent selling office fee. Typically it is 1 to 2 percent.
Listing Flat Fee (MLS Participation)	Instead of a percentage the listing office charges a flat fee anywhere from $500 to $2,900 or more plus 3 percent to the selling office.
Fee Is a Percentage of Sale Price (No MLS Participation)	Typically 3 percent or less since you don't have MLS cooperation. Buyers come through the listing office efforts only.
Flat Fee (No MLS Participation)	Brokerage charges a flat fee and does not participate on the MLS. Typical charges are $2,900 plus or minus, depending on the area and price range.
Full Service with In-House Sale Discount	If listing office finds the buyer they'll pass the savings on to you. Typically, you'll save 1 to 2 percent of the sale price.

market is like in your area. If it's a hot market and all you have to do is put out a sign and the offers flow, then paying 6 percent may not be money well spent.

A slow market, in contrast, is a different ball game. In a slow market, you'll need all the help you can get, and having your home listed on the MLS is a plus. Additionally, qualified buyers are harder to find, and having an experienced agent on your side can be a big help with a messy offer.

Negotiating Commission Rates

Here again we're walking into sticky emotional territory. Sellers want the best deal, and agents want to be paid for their efforts. Can there be a common ground? Probably, and here are some suggestions that can help you keep as much equity as possible.

■ If you don't want to be bothered by the sales process—if negotiating with strangers, showing your home yourself, and handling the paperwork doesn't appeal to you —then going with a full-service Realtor is likely your best option. A half-hearted attempt to sell on your own can cost you money.

■ If it's a hot market and putting up a sign results in multiple offers, then approach an agent with an offer to pay only for doing the paperwork. A fee ranging from $500 to 1 percent of the sales price is reasonable for this, depending on the complexity. Also check with an attorney and find out what she would charge to do the paperwork; it may be a lot less.

■ Offer to list for the full commission, with the stipulation that if you find the buyer the commission is reduced to a putting-the-deal-together fee. This is sometimes called an exclusive agency listing, and if the buyer comes through the listing office or MLS, you owe the commission. In a sense, you're gambling on who comes up with the buyer first.

■ Suppose you have buyers interested in your home but they have to sell their home first or have some problems they have to clear up. Because you don't want to lose valuable selling time waiting for an iffy situation to get resolved, you decide to also list your home. What happens if your interested buyers come through after you've already signed the paperwork. Do you have to pay a commission on your buyer?

The easiest solution is to simply write on the listing agreement that the following parties (list by name and address) are exempt. Most agents will want to put a 30-day time limit on the exemption. But, if one of the exempted parties comes through during that time, you've saved a commission. If not, you haven't lost anything.

■ If it's a buyer's market, you'll need all the exposure you can get. Plus, buyers tend to come in with low offers, and a good agent can make the difference between a deal that flies and one that doesn't. In this situation you'll want the best agent you can find, and that means paying 6 percent. Also, a good agent has the experience and savvy to squeeze more out of a counter than you may otherwise get.

■ In a hot market, going with a flat-fee, non-MLS brokerage can be a good way to shave costs. Obviously, you won't need MLS exposure if buyers are trolling the neighborhoods looking for newly planted *For Sale* signs.

Whether you sign a listing or go FSBO, a hot topic that has garnered a lot of recent press coverage is property disclosure. How to protect yourself is the next step in understanding the paperwork.

All About Seller Disclosure Forms

Most states now have a clause in the listing agreement that you agree to disclose to the listing agent any problems the house may have and fill out a property condition disclosure. This means selling homes "as is" is getting more difficult and you do so at your peril.

Horror stories abound of home buyers suing the seller for problems they find after moving in. While you may never be able to completely insulate yourself from post-sale problems, you can minimize the risk with good disclosures.

In one case, sellers who sold their 40-year-old remodeled bungalow went the extra mile to make sure the home was problem free. They had a professional inspector look at the home, and then they fixed the few minor problems he found.

The home looked great and sold the first week it was on the market. The sellers bought a new home and moved in immediately, leaving their previous home vacant for the month it took to close. The buyers, Dale and Janelle, got a copy of the inspection report at the time they made their offer in addition to a four-page sellers disclosure. During move-in, Janelle turned on the tub and another faucet to flush out the drains but got distracted for a few minutes and let the water run. Later when she went downstairs, she found to her horror a foot of water in the basement. Water had backed up through a floor drain in the laundry and flooded the finished basement.

A plumber that checked out the line to the street found roots from a tree, which had been removed years ago, had invaded the sewer pipe and created a partial obstruction. That, coupled with soap scum hardening in the line when the home sat vacant for a month, narrowed it even further. Normal water flow of a toilet or faucet was not a problem, but the partially blocked line couldn't handle the large volume from the two faucets opened full. It was a problem the sellers couldn't have foreseen.

Damage was considerable, with soaked Sheetrock, carpets, and some furniture. Low bid to fix the damage topped $12,000. The buyers were upset and felt the sellers should pay. The sellers didn't think they were responsible because they had disclosed everything they knew about the home on the disclosure forms and furnished a property inspection. It was a tense situation headed for court. Luckily, that never happened. Both buyers and sellers agreed to arbitration. In the end the insurance company covered most of the damage, and the sellers paid the $500 deductible.

The bottom line is, although the sellers ended up paying $500 it could have been worse. The inspection report and disclosure forms clearly showed the sellers sold in good faith and didn't attempt to cover up a problem. This defused an emotionally charged situation and avoided potentially expensive litigation.

Property Disclosure Forms

Sellers' property condition disclosure forms vary slightly from state to state, but the basics are the same. They are typically two- to five-page forms with mostly yes/no questions that cover the home's components. The purchase agreement may also have a time limit written in for delivering the completed disclosure to the buyers. The buyers in turn have to sign that they received a copy.

You can go to *www.sid-davis.com* and download a sample disclosure form in PDF format.

If you're going FSBO, it's in your best interests to take this form seriously and make sure you get copies with all signatures.

Other important disclosures are the federal lead-based-paint forms, which have some real teeth in them.

If Your Home Was Build Prior to 1978

The federal government now requires that all homes build prior to 1978 must include the following paperwork to protect buyers from lead-based paint:

1. You must give the buyer the EPA pamphlet, *Protect Your Family from Lead in Your Home.*

2. You need to fill out a lead-based-paint disclosure form. If there's no lead-based paint in the home, you check the appropriate box and sign at the bottom along with the buyers.

3. If there's a possible lead-based hazard, you'll need to use an addendum giving the buyers ten days to do a professional inspection. The offer and sale then become subject to the terms of the lead-based-paint addendum.

You can download the EPA lead-based pamphlet from *www.epa.gov/opptintr/lead/leadpdfe* in PDF format.

A lead-based-paint disclosure form can be downloaded from *www.sid-davis.com* in PDF format.

In one particular case, when a seller didn't give the buyer the necessary lead-based-paint forms, the buyer used this omission to walk away from the deal a week later after getting cold feet. Even though the home didn't have a lead-based-paint problem, it was built prior to 1978, which made it subject to federal paperwork. You can get these forms from a local office supply, a friendly Realtor, or check your state's real estate division's Web sites.

One of the most important things you can do to increase the size of your closing check is make sure your home is in good selling condition. Things to do and traps to avoid are covered in the next chapter.

CHAPTER 2

Prep Your Home to Sell for More

Home sellers who spend a little time and effort making their homes more marketable will net thousands of dollars more than the homeowner who pushes an 18 by 24 inch, red and white, plastic *For Sale* sign in the turf and calls it a day.

Selling a house is very similar to selling a car. For example, take someone who wants to sell an SUV and buy a better model. Likely he will put a lot of energy into cleaning the inside and carefully applying a protective coat to the vinyl or leather interior. The chrome wheels shine from having been cleaned with fine steel wool and metal cleaner, tires are sporting a shiny black coat, the engine compartment is degreased and looks spotless, and an air freshener is hung from the inside mirror. Many owners even prepare a history of oil changes and service work as proof the car has been lovingly cared for.

Why do they do this? Because they know competition is stiff. There are lots of vehicles on the market, shined and pampered just like his. But most important, the owner's goal is to get as much money as possible. He's researched the market and knows the price down to the nearest dollar. If all goes right, maybe he can get anywhere from a few hundred to a couple of thousand dollars more than he would if he traded in the car.

Similarly, you should approach selling a home much like selling a prized SUV—only instead of trying to make a few hundred to a couple of thousand extra dollars, you're working to increase your closing check by tens of thousands of dollars.

Selling your home is not astrophysics, it just takes knowing what to do and focusing on doing it. Whether you plan on working with an agent or selling on your own, this book lays out a road map with the shortcuts clearly marked. You will not only have fun selling your home, you'll end up with the biggest closing check possible in the shortest time.

To get started, let's take a look at home equity and the two ways it increases.

It's All About Equity

When you're selling your home, you're looking to get the most equity possible. In a way equity is your closing check—what you walk away with after the deal. It's the sales price after subtracting the selling costs and the mortgage balance.

Equity, as the real estate types call it, grows by a combination of paying down (*amortization*) the mortgage balance each month and the house going up in value (*appreciation*). If you're one of the unlucky sellers who end up with the selling costs and a mortgage balance larger than the sales price, you've got negative equity. That means that at closing you'll have to write a check rather than deposit one.

Amortization

Of the two types of equity, amortization is the least important in the short term. That's because in the early years of a 30-year loan just about all the payment goes toward interest.

Because so little of the payment goes to paying down the principle, it takes several years before there is a significant increase in equity. For example, a 30-year mortgage for $180,000 at 6 percent interest will only pay down the loan by $2,210 the first year, and by $29,366 after ten years.

Appreciation

The second equity builder, appreciation, is a lot more exciting. You make money by your home going up in value.

To give you an idea how quickly a home's value can increase from appreciation, suppose home values in your area went up 4 percent in the last year. If you bought your house last year for $200,000, your home has appreciated $8,000 ($200,000 × 4 percent). In that same year, you may have only paid down the mortgage a few thousand dollars, even with a low interest rate. In some urban areas, homes have appreciated more than 4 percent a month, which would make the difference even greater.

As you can see, appreciation is the key to making big bucks, so you want to do all you can to take advantage of it. Lucky for you, there are things you can do to help your house appreciate. Part of appreciation depends on the value of homes in your neighborhood. If, for example, crime goes down, school performance goes up, or commuting suddenly becomes easier, the value of your home will appreciate. But these things are hard to control.

Another part of appreciation is the condition and appeal of your home. If your home is in excellent condition and "feels" like a home, people will pay more for it. And that's the key to selling your home for the most money possible—making sure your home appeals to buyers on an emotional level. There are buyers who will pay top dollar for a home and the next section shows you how to attract these types of buyers with the least amount of money and pain.

Increasing Your Home's Value 101

Few things are more controversial among Realtors, remodelers, decorators, and appraisers than which upgrades add value and which ones are a waste of money. It can be a difficult call because you're trying to predict what colors and decor a total stranger will like. And no matter what you do, some people will like what you've done and some won't.

In one instance, a Realtor advised her clients to install new carpet, replace aging fixtures, and give the kitchen a make-over. The sellers spent about $35,000 to make their home "more saleable."

In the end, the home ended up selling close to asking price, but before the buyers moved in they tore out and remodeled the kitchen and replaced the carpets and floor coverings. Obviously, the new buyers didn't like the previous owners' decorating taste.

This brings up some interesting questions: Were the seller's upgrades wasted in this case? Would the buyers have bought the home without the upgrades, and would they have paid the same price? Who knows for sure. It's possible the new owners had gone through a home show the week before closing and saw their dream kitchen they couldn't live without.

Improvements That Pay, Improvements That Don't

There are three types of home improvements: the first adds to or maintains the value of your home; it's a good type and wears a white hat.

The second makes your home a better house and more saleable, but it doesn't always increase the value significantly; that still makes it a good guy in a white hat. The third type costs you money and wears a black hat; it doesn't add value or make your home more saleable and sometimes it can lower the value or make your home harder to sell.

The important thing to remember is that the super-charged, mega-horsepower engine powering home sales is emotion. When buyers look at a bunch of homes and none exactly fits their mental picture of what they would be happy living in, they'll go into "can we redo this to get what we want" mode. Even though your home may need updating, if the charm and potential are there and buyers can visualize it becoming their dream home, then you'll likely get a good offer.

Of course, price range is also a critical factor. If buyers are stretching financially to get into a home, their focus will be more on finding a house that won't need much improvement when they move in. But, on the other hand, if they're moving up into their second home, then location, charm, and condition become high on the list.

Let the Area Guide You

Unfortunately, you don't have a crystal ball to peer into to know what buyers are thinking, so you have to go by what type of buyers the homes in your area are attracting.

For example, in a particular subdivision nine out of twelve sales only went through when the sellers agreed to pay part of the closing costs to help buyers qualify. As a result, when the agent worked up pricing for a listing in this area, he pointed this out to the sellers and prepared them for this type of offer.

Sure enough, two weeks later an offer came in requesting the owners pay $3,200 toward the buyer's closing costs. The sellers were prepared for this and had a counter offer ready. The counter was eagerly accepted and the deal closed a few weeks later.

If your area is more upscale and attracts move-up home buyers, then condition can become more critical. Many buyers can't or won't visualize what your home would look like if changes were made. For them, it's easier to go to the next home on the list than to strain neurons visualizing new carpets or paint colors.

True, there are a few buyers who are decorator- or color savvy. But, in the real world you want to market to the 90 percent—the average buyers. It's marketing suicide to use your advertising resources trying to attract the few who may or may not consider your home as-is. In other words, if vanilla is the best-selling ice cream, why try to sell bubble gum pistachio!

How to Determine What to Upgrade and Save Big Bucks

Before you fall into the expensive trap of blindly replacing carpet and new kitchen cabinets, there are three things you can do to save a lot of work and a few thousand dollars.

First, check out the competition. If you have a Realtor, ask her to run a list of homes similar to yours that are for sale in the area. If you don't have a Realtor, you should seriously consider using one. They could save you a lot of time, hassle, and money, and in a transaction as big as this you really want a professional on your side. If you want to try going it alone, access the multiple listing service (MLS) at *www .realtor.com* and look for homes in your area. These are the homes that buyers are looking at and comparing your home to.

Second, go through these homes and look at them as if you were a buyer. Be objective: think like a buyer, take lots of notes, and use the handy comparison chart in Figure 2-1.

Remodeling Magazine publishes a yearly *Cost vs. Value Report* on their Web site—*www.remodeling magazine.com*—which lists what percentage of the cost of upgrades you can expect to recoup in different areas. *Realtor* magazine also publishes this report on their Web site: *www .realtor.org/realtormag.*

Third, notice what upgrades the competition has that your home doesn't have. Keep in mind that you don't want to be a lot better, just a little bit better. Otherwise, you risk over-improving your home for the area and wasting time and money. You need to spend only enough money to give you an edge.

Examples of overkill are putting in high-end countertops like Corian or granite when other homes in your price range have laminate, or upgrading floors to wood or tile when other homes have vinyl, and so on.

A home comparison worksheet (Figure 2-1) can also give you a feel for which improvements you'll need to make to be competitive. After you've completed the worksheet, make a list of the items you'll need to improve along with cost estimates. This will probably require a trip to the nearest home improvement center to get prices.

For items that need professional installation, like floors, cabinets, and countertops, get three bids and compare them for the best deal.

FIGURE 2-1
Home comparison worksheet.

Compare each item on the list in your home to the three homes in your area that are most similar to yours. Be objective as possible and give each item a score of 1 to 5.

Item	Your Home	Home #1	Home #2	Home #3
Neighborhood				
Curb Appeal from Across the Street				
Landscaping				
Curb Appeal from the Street to the Front Door				
Entryway				
First Impression as You Walk Through the Front Door				
Condition of the Walls				
Condition of Carpets and Floors				
Kitchen: First Impression				
Kitchen Cabinets				
Kitchen Appliances and Fixtures				
Kitchen Lighting				
Kitchen Dining Area (Size)				
Family Room				
Bedrooms and Closets (Number and Size)				
Baths (First Impression)				
Bath Fixtures				
Bath off Master Bedroom				
Garage (Size and Neatness)				
Overall Exterior Condition (Siding)				
Roof (Condition and Age)				

What Buyers Expect to Be in Good Condition

In addition to indoor plumbing, there are some things buyers expect to be in good condition before they'll even consider the home. To put your home at the top of the food chain consider the following:

■ *Painting.* This is the number one improvement you can do to make your home more appealing. It's almost a cliché, but an eggshell finish or white with just a tint of beige is still the best color. Go with a high-quality paint, it's not only easier to apply but it looks better too. Going with off-white walls makes your home look bigger and helps the buyers visualize their pictures and their furniture in your house. When that happens, it's more money in your pocket.

■ *Furnace/Air Conditioner.* Buyers expect a home to have reasonably new and working heating and cooling systems. If your system has a problem, fix it before showing the home.

■ *Roof.* Buyers expect a home to have a water-tight, problem-free roof. If it has problems, replace or fix it before putting the home on the market. If the roof is ten years old or older, get a roof inspection from a licensed roofing contractor. Make sure the inspection report states clearly about how many years the roof is good for. Should a buyer ask about the roof, you'll have the paperwork to back you up.

■ *Floor Coverings.* If you have to replace carpet or vinyl, go with a neutral color that goes with about anything. If you've gone through the competition's homes, you'll know exactly where you stand on this item.

■ *Kitchen Cabinets.* One successful husband and wife home rehab team who buys, fixes up, and sells several homes a year rarely replaces kitchen cabinets. They carefully sand the cabinets and paint them with a high gloss white paint or stain and refinish the wood if it's in good condition. There are lots of options to replacing them.

■ *Exterior.* Look for and fix damaged *gutters, exterior sheathing, concrete, garage doors,* and so on. You can count on buyers walking around your house with a critical eye.

■ *Appliances.* Replace any appliances that look worn or are at the end of their service life.

■ *Interior Surfaces.* If the interior paint is still in good condition, wash the walls and other surfaces with a good household cleaner. Better yet, hiring a cleaning service for this project can be worth it, especially if you've got high or vaulted ceilings.

Many homes are sold by word-of-mouth from neighbors. If your home has a reputation for being in great condition, you may get a quick sale as soon as everyone sees the sign go up.

Arnold and Nikki sold their home this way when they put their "Mrs. Clean lives here" six-year-old two-story colonial on the market. A neighbor told her friend at work, who had a sister looking for a home. The neighbor so raved about the home, how well it was maintained, and how clean it was that the home buyers were nearly presold. They made a full-price offer after a quick walk-through.

On the other hand, if you're "Mr. Clean-challenged" you'll need to do some work to bring the home up to selling condition. Hiring a home cleaning service to do the job is an investment that is certain to pay off with a better offer. Two interesting home cleaning Web sites are *cleaning.com* and *merrymaids.com*.

If you also have a clutter problem—which many homeowners have—you may also consider calling an organization consultant who works with homeowners to bring clutter under control. Check out the phone directory—under organizing products and services—for consultants.

Of course, once your home is in top condition you'll want to invite as many people through as possible so you can get a buzz going about how nice your home looks.

Improvements That Help Sell

The next improvement category deals with those things that help sell a home, but which don't necessarily increase its value. Usually you haven't wasted the money spent on the improvements, you've been able to enjoy them, and in a slow market they may have made the difference between the home selling and not selling.

Improvements that fall into this category can differ from area to area, but the most common are:

■ Upgraded appliances that other homes in your price range don't have. In one starter home, the owner loved to cook and had installed a $2,000 Viking gas range. Did it increase the value of the house? No, but it made the kitchen stand out in the buyers' minds and tipped the scales enough to get an offer. Again, you don't want to overdo it, but think about items that don't cost a lot, but that are unique.

■ Small add-ons that blend in well, such as a greenhouse or solar-ium, extra carport, or wood-burning stove.

■ Upgraded fencing, automatic sprinkler system, landscaping, newly planted trees, and other landscaping pluses.

■ A double garage is a big plus, but in many areas won't increase the value a 100 percent of the cost. A second garage will return even less, but can be a big sales advantage when the buyer is a woodworker, mechanic, space-intensive hobbyist, or owns an RV or boat. For them this can be a prime motivator to make an offer.

Typically, if most of the homes in your neighborhood have garages and yours doesn't, it's going to hurt. Adding a garage when most of the homes in your area don't have one will help sell the home, but recouping the cost can be difficult.

■ Any interior improvements that other similar homes don't have, such as oak railings, three-tone paint, top-of-the line carpeting or vinyl, more expensive light fixtures and windows, and so on.

To avoid going over the top in costs, check out similar homes for sale and go to open houses in the area to see what upgrades are popular.

How Over-Improving Can Cost You

This category wears the black hat. You spend a lot of money only to find out when you try to sell, there's a problem. You discover you not only can't recover your investment, but the improvements prevent your home from selling.

Sometimes there's a fine line between improvements that help sell and those that make your house unsaleable, as one couple found out when they tried to sell.

When Jamie and Susan decided to sell the home they had lived in for the past nine years, they added the cost of the improvements they had made to their sales price. They felt the $60,000 they spent adding a new roof, kitchen, and family room increased their home's value by the same amount.

Unfortunately, when they made their improvements they didn't consider what other homes in the neighborhood were selling for since they planned on living in their home forever. But when Jamie lost his job in a company downsizing and had to relocate, they had no choice but to put the home on the market.

Susan called a Realtor whose name was on several *For Sale* signs in the area, and asked her to come over to talk about selling their home. When the agent arrived she showed them a list of homes that had sold in the area the last ninety days. She then told them that since the area was basically a first-time homeowner neighborhood, their improvements would probably only add about $12,000 to the home's value.

Understandably, Susan was upset with the Realtor's numbers and decided to get a second opinion. One of her neighbors had moved in a few months ago, so she called and got their agent's number and called him to come and look at their house.

After also looking at what homes had sold for in the neighborhood, the second agent's pricing opinion was similar to that of the first agent. However, he felt it would take about forty-five days longer to sell.

So how could $60,000 in improvements add so little to a home's value? It's all about the neighborhood and area. Here's often why:

■ Homes in the area that are similar tend to attract home buyers who qualify for that narrow price range. If you improve out of that price bracket, you're in trouble.

For example, if homes in the area are selling for $130,000 and a home goes on the market for $180,000, it's not likely to attract buyers for that price range: Those buyers are looking to buy in $180,000 neighborhoods. Also, most buyers who look in the $130,000 neighborhood can't qualify for an additional $50,000 to buy an over-improved home. As a result, the home will sit on the market unsold—a white elephant.

■ It's unlikely an over-improved home will appraise for what the owners have spent, because appraisers look at neighborhood sale averages to establish value.

■ If the neighborhood has problems, the improvements won't count as much. Negative factors, such as proximity to freeways/ramps, noise or bad smells from nearby commercial activity, or other environmental negatives, cause values to drop. As a result, any improvements will be for naught.

The same is true if the view from the neighborhood is not desirable. Homes may face a busy road, factory, railroad tracks, or eroded gully. Also, if it's an area of older homes that have deteriorated because pride of ownership is lacking and/or there are a significant number of rentals, home prices will be lower.

What Happens if You Don't Fix It Up

This is also an option, but the results can get ugly and will almost always cost you big time. For example, one home-selling couple who moved to another state refused to do the upgrades needed to make their home competitive. They had painted each room a different bright color and the carpets were left dirty. In fact, the whole house needed a thorough cleaning.

As a result, the home languished on the market for months with lots of showings but no offers. Unfortunately for the sellers, the mortgage clock kept ticking, costing them over $1,000 a month.

When they finally did get an offer, it was 10 months later and it barely covered their closing costs. They had paid out over $16,000 in mortgage payments and utility costs and had drained their equity to zero.

The irony is that had the sellers spent about $1,700 in painting and cleanup before putting the home on the market, they could have walked away with some big bucks to put down on their next home.

Hopefully, you've now got a good idea of which improvements help and which ones cost you. The next step is to look at your home's curb appeal. How does it stack up against the competition?

Importance of Curb Appeal

We've all heard you have just seconds to make a good impression or the opportunity is gone forever. This is also true when selling your house. You mess up the first chance and you may not get another opportunity.

The first impression your house gives a buyer who drives slowly by is what real estate people call *curb appeal*. If you have great curb appeal, the sale is half done. If you don't, the buyer is wondering what else is not up to par. And in their mind the value takes an escalator ride down.

The buyers' first impressions will color everything they see. If it's not good, they'll be looking for problems and mentally subtracting flaws and worn items from your asking price. This ends up putting you on the defensive trying to justify your asking price to skeptical buyers.

How One Couple Did It Right

When Travis and Danielle had twin girls, the starter home they bought five years ago suddenly became too small. They wanted to build a new home nearby but knew they would have to get top dollar and a fast sale on their existing home to make it work. So they set about doing just that.

The first project they tackled was curb appeal, making their home as attractive as possible to drive-bys. This is what they did:

■ The roof was getting old, but fortunately it had only one layer of asphalt shingles so that a complete tear-off of the old layer wasn't necessary. So, Travis and a few friends spent a weekend adding a new layer of twenty-year shingles. This improved the look considerably.

■ Next, the sellers removed the run-away bushes growing along the foundation and replaced them with neat flower beds of geraniums, petunias, marigolds, and impatiens. Other flower beds were created around the birch trees that framed the house, giving the front yard a lot of eye-catching color.

■ Since the exterior was fifty-year-old brick, Travis rented a high-pressure sprayer and washed the exterior thoroughly, getting rid of decades of old grime. He also gave the driveway a good cleaning to get rid of the oil and rust stains. The house never looked better.

■ Finally, the lawn was given a dose of nitrogen-rich fertilizer to keep it at maximum green for the next few weeks.

Travis and Danielle had already painted the inside and cleaned the carpets, so the next steps were to put an ad in the local paper and a *For Sale* sign on the lawn. Almost immediately people stopped by to see the home. It was in a good neighborhood, and starter-priced homes in great condition are hard to find in any market. So, it's not surprising the action was heavy.

The second couple that came through made a full-price offer on the spot. The sellers wondered whether they had priced the home too low, but realizing that it probably wouldn't appraise for more, they accepted the offer.

The seller's efforts had paid off because they had taken the time to make the outside as appealing as possible. Buyers were half-sold before they got to the front door.

In retrospect, what had Travis and Danielle done right?

1. In upgrading they made sure every dollar they spent multiplied many times in increasing its value. They chose carefully the improvements that would enhance the value, such as new laminate counter tops, replacing old single-pane with vinyl double-pane windows, and restoring the wood floors.

2. All improvements were consistent with the neighborhood. In other words, they knew not to install expensive granite counter tops or top-of-the-line appliances in a starter neighborhood.

3. The goal they worked for was to make the home look fresh, crisp, and ready to move into so the buyers wouldn't have to do anything.

4. They checked out what other homes had sold for in the area and talked to an appraiser, so they knew about how high they could price their home.

The bottom line is this: Too many homeowners prolong the sale and lose thousands of dollars because they don't make their home attractive to buyers' first impressions.

How to Improve Your Curb Appeal

The first step is to walk across the street from your home and pretend you're a buyer. It can be hard to be objective since it's your hearth and home, so having your agent, a trusted friend, or a relative along helps.

What do you see that detracts from good curb appeal? Take notes and/or photos. Look at other homes in your area that you find attractive. Note what they've done and also what you can do to enhance your curb appeal.

Paul and Lanez did this when they decided to sell and move to a new subdivision nearby. Looking at their home from across the street, they tried to put themselves in a buyer's shoes and looked at their home as if they were seeing it for the first time. It didn't take long before reality started to sink in. They were amazed at how overgrown their yard had become.

The five-foot trees they planted a few years ago had grown tall and spread out, nearly obscuring the house. Foundation plants were above the windowsills and out of control. Clearly, this would discourage home buyers driving by from stopping and going through the home. Obviously, they would need to spend a Saturday morning with a power saw and trimmer to tame the wilderness.

In this case, the sellers swung into action, rented a chipper that shreds limbs, borrowed a chain saw from their neighbor, and sharpened their hedge trimmer. It took several hours of hard work but the result was amazing. Paul and Lanez cleared the trees that blocked the front of the house and trimmed the privet hedges down to about 42 inches. All the limbs and trimmings went through the chipper and were turned into mulch.

The house, now framed by the remaining trees and the neatly trimmed hedges, created an image of a well-maintained home—exactly what's needed to give buyers the impression this is a home worth going through.

Tips for Choosing Exterior Paint Colors

If your home's exterior is worn or faded, you'll need to paint or install a new exterior. Picking the right colors is important. With color you can highlight the house's features and give it strong appeal. For instance, how do you think a Queen Anne style home with its ornate facade and lots of trim would look if everything were painted one color? You'll find that for such homes and other homes with strong architectural styles, contrasting colors are the norm.

If you drive around looking at homes that are attractive, you'll notice that many attractive exteriors are a combination of the darker and lighter versions of the same color. Notice how color breaks up the exterior and highlights the details.

Some additional tips for choosing exterior colors are:

- Stay away from the bright primary colors and instead look for muted hues for siding and trim.

- Dark colors usually make a house look smaller, while lighter colors reflect light and make it appear larger. This is perhaps the reason why pale yellow or white houses with contrasting trim seem to sell better than those with dominant darker colors.

- Look at sample colors in both direct sunlight and shade. Bright colors can appear washed out in direct sunlight.

- When you find a color you like, buy a quart and test it on a section of the wall or trim and under different light conditions.

- Start with the dominant color first, usually that of the siding or roof, before you select the trim or accent colors.

- Look at other homes that are similar to yours and notice what you like and don't like. If your home is an architectural classic—such as a Salt Box, Cape Cod, or Craftsman bungalow—you can find attractive color schemes in books and videos at your library.

■ If your home looks dated or boring, you may consider hiring a contractor to give your exterior a makeover by upgrading or adding trim and accents. You'll need to watch your costs carefully and do some homework so you don't get carried away and spend more than you'll get back.

Referring often to your list of repairs needed and their approximate cost will keep you from "improvement creep" or getting carried away in the excitement of upgrading.

One seller who started painting and upgrading the trim felt he needed to add new siding too so that everything would look new. He ended up paying over $20,000. Unfortunately, in his neighborhood there was no way he could recoup those costs when he sold.

So, don't forget to do some homework first and set a limit on how much money you can spend. Use the checklist in Figure 2-2 as a handy guide to get started.

Beyond Curb Appeal: The Emotional Factors

Whatever you want to call them—subliminal cues, positive vibes, or subconscious attraction—emotional factors are often what causes buyers to make a decision to buy or reject a certain house. Colors, smells, memories of a home they grew up in, a desire to have something better than their friends, and images of how happy they would be living there are all emotional triggers. And the more positive emotional triggers that fire, the better they'll like your home.

Many times a buyer will walk through the door and immediately know this is the house they've been looking for. They see it. They feel it. Their excitement grows as they walk through the home mentally picturing their furniture in the family room and their pictures on the walls. Emotional triggers are firing away like a twenty-one gun salute. This phenomenon exists not only with first-time home buyers, but buyers who have bought several homes and know the routine.

This is the type of buyer you want to attract. They're looking for their dream home. They're shopping on emotion and price is secondary. When they find their home a fast decision is the norm.

In one case, Angie had gone through nine on their list of twelve homes. Most were not even close to what she was looking for. Two were possibilities, but since the vibes were not quite right those homes went on the back burner for a possible second inspection if nothing better turned up.

FIGURE 2-2
How to increase your home's curb appeal.

Item	Action Needed
Roof	Buyers who offer top dollar assume the roof will be in good condition. If the shingles curl, are brittle, and break easily you may have to replace them.
Siding	If brick or vinyl/aluminum, pressure wash with mild detergent. Replace any damaged sections. If the trim and siding are faded you'll need to paint.
Trees	Typically, trees should frame the house, not obscure it. Sometimes large trees along the parking strip define the neighborhood and add to its appeal. The key is trim enough so buyers can see the front of your home.
Landscaping	Trim all trees and bushes from the front of the home. If they can't see it, they'll keep driving. Plant foundation flowers and trim hedges. The key is to scale existing plants to complement the house. Cut and edge lawns. Add fertilizer if needed to green the lawn.
Driveway and Walkways	Steam or pressure clean to remove oil and rust stains. Replace damaged concrete.
Entryway	Sand and paint or replace any railing in bad condition as well as the entry door. Don't forget the porch light fixture, polish or replace if needed. Also, make sure the doorbell works and is attractive.
Porch	Fix or replace damaged concrete steps and deck. This is the route buyers take to your front door. You can't afford a negative perception this early in the showing process. Depending on the season, put flower boxes and planters near the entrance.
Garage Door	Paint and repair garage door if needed. Add a garage door opener if you don't have one. It's a big plus for buyers to click the opener and have a door power up showing a spotless garage.

The tenth home on her list was an older brick Tudor that had been extensively updated and was at the top of her price range. As she parked across the street she was immediately captivated by the home's charm. The landscaping fit the style with huge sycamores framing the home. Lawn and flower beds were well cared for and neatly edged. Even the Kelly-green entry door looked new and inviting.

The walk from the street to the front door got her emotional juices flowing, and she was half sold by the time she pushed the antique brass doorbell button. Yes, even the doorbell was attractive and working!

Not surprisingly, she ended up offering close to the full price for the home. She couldn't do anything less because she had fallen in love with the house . . . it was her dream home and it had fired all her emotional bullets. At that point price was not her biggest consideration—making a deal was.

Creating Emotional Appeal

Some ideas for giving your home more emotional appeal are:

■ Give the interior a fresh coat of neutral paint. Yes, the decorator magazines have great-looking rooms with lots of color. Since there's no way you can predict a buyer's taste in color, going with a light, neutral color is safe. Too many homes languish on the market or get low offers when the sellers' egos get in the way. For example, they may feel anyone whose decorating choices are different from theirs are peasants and aren't worthy to buy their home.

■ Make sure the carpets are clean. If it's been a few years since you've replaced the carpets, go with a neutral color and/or pattern. Wood floors should be refinished if needed.

■ The home should look as if Mr. Clean lives there. Any area of your home that doesn't sparkle will distract, and you don't want the buyer's attention to shift from thinking about owning the home to noticing the problems. And when buyers' thinking switches into problem mode and they start finding fault, you're not going to get the price you want.

A excellent book and video on how to create emotional appeal and get your home ready to show is *Dress your House for Success* by Martha Webb and Sarah Parsons Zackheim, at *www.bcwvideo.com* or 800-288-4635. Another great video is *How To Prepare Your House for Sale*, at *www.barb.net* or 800-392-7161.

■ Make sure the colors and textures flow and carry from one room to another. For instance, if buyers encounter too big a color or decor shift going from the entry to the family room, it can create an uncomfortable feeling and result in a quick exit.

■ Remove extra furniture, photos, pictures, and anything that will detract a buyer from trying to visualize their stuff in the home. Yes, that applies to any trophies that will catch a buyer's attention, such as a twelve-pound bass you caught on a two-pound test line for a Northern Hemisphere record.

The next step in the sales process is to keep those emotional triggers firing by making sure the rest of your home lives up to the buyer's first impression. Just like in a who-done-it mystery, you want the suspense to build.

How a House Smells: A Big Emotional Trigger

How often have you walked into a restaurant, home, or business and been ambushed by an unpleasant odor? What was your reaction? Was that bad smell forever after linked to that business site or home?

Even though your home can be the most visually appealing habitat within a hundred light years, if it smells like month-old roadkill it won't even get to the playoffs. Strong odors can be a big turnoff for many buyers. Since you're trying to get buyers emotionally involved with your home, how your home smells can be a critical factor.

You live with the odors in your home every day and so don't notice them. Some usual problems are odors from diapers, smoking, dirty laundry, cooking, or pets. The best way to find out is have a neighbor (trusted) or relative walk through the home for a smell test.

Olfactory items to keep in mind are:

■ Many people are sensitive to pet odors or allergic to pet hair. If you have pets, make sure the litter box is clean and out of sight. Also, make arrangements for a neighbor to take your pet during showing. You may love your cat, dog, or other life form, but others may not.

■ If the home has been vacant or closed up, it can develop less than ideal smells. Using carpet and other deodorizers can solve this problem.

■ Cooking odors can also be a problem. Not everyone likes curry, cabbage, onions, or strong spices. The safe approach is to vent the home well and use spray deodorizers before showing.

- Don't burn candles inside the home. They leave a black smoke residue on the upper walls and ceilings. If you like the smell of scented candles, buy a small hot plate designed for heating candles so they give off the scent without a flame.

- Install stick-on or plug-in scent dispensers around the house to give it a fresh and inviting smell. But don't use too many dispensers or mix scents, or you may create a smell you don't want.

In one particular instance a nice home languished on the market for months because the owners loved to cook with curry and the odor permeated the house. They had become insensitive to the strong spice's odor and couldn't understand why everyone who toured the home commented on the odor and left quickly. Unfortunately, the sellers refused to change their cooking habits or do a thorough deodorizing. It wasn't long before agents wouldn't even show the home and eventually it went into foreclosure.

Clutter Can Kill a Sale

Another sale-killer is clutter. Many sellers have a hard time realizing that the way you live in a house is different from the way you sell it.

For example, one seller had decorated her home with nicknacks, stuffed animals, and antiques that covered just about every square foot. It was a showroom, museum, and picture gallery all in one.

Showing the home was a challenge. Potential buyers got so enthralled by the "stuff" that they got sidetracked and forgot they were buying a home, not accessory shopping. As weeks turned in months it became obvious that the home wasn't going to sell with all the distractions. Buyers were not identifying with the house. They couldn't picture themselves living there so it was on to the next home on their list.

The listing agent had talked to the seller several times about removing and boxing everything up but she refused. Finally, her husband, who had been transferred to another state, came home for a few days and everyone got together for a summit.

It wasn't easy, but the seller's agent finally got her clients to see the reality of the situation. She had them rent a large storage shed and move everything but the bare essentials out of the house.

Next, they hired a professional painter to patch all the holes in the walls from the shelves and hangers and paint the interior an eggshell white. They then had the carpets cleaned and hired a professional cleaning crew to come in and clean the house.

What a difference! It wasn't the same house. The listing Realtor e-mailed the agents who had shown the home previously and attached photos showing the difference. She was able to jump-start some showing activity and the home sold about three weeks later.

How to Declutter

In making your home emotionally appealing, decluttering is a critical component. Some suggestions on how to get started are:

- Remove family photos from walls and stairwells. You want the buyer to imagine their photos and not be distracted by yours.

- Leave only the minimum amount of furniture in each room. This makes the rooms look larger. Buyers can more easily picture their own furniture in the room and not be distracted.

- Kitchen counters should be clean and free of appliances and utensils.

- If you have a hutch or other furniture items that crowd the kitchen, relocate or store them. It's critical to make the kitchen look as big as possible.

- The refrigerator shouldn't look like a bulletin board. Remove all the sticky notes, magnets, and school art work.

- If the lighting fixtures are dated, replace them. Otherwise make sure the fixtures have the maximum wattage and number of bulbs possible. The more light, the better your home shows.

- Don't forget to clean out closets. Some buyers find peeking in them irresistible, and you don't want to dampen their enthusiasm with clutter. Clean and empty closets appear larger and won't trigger negative impressions.

With your home about ready to go on the market, there's one more thing you want to avoid that trips up many sellers.

Putting a Home on the Market Too Soon Attracts the Wrong Buyers

One big mistake many sellers make is putting their home on the market before it's ready. They get over-eager, don't realize the importance of prepping their home, or don't want to expend the effort. This results in a big waste of time and resources. Here are four reasons why:

First, you don't want to lose the pool of buyers in your price range who might be interested in your home if they were to see it at its best. If they reject it and move on you'll most likely lose them to the competition because they're looking to buy now.

Second, if you attract buyers who are looking for a reason to low-ball your price, you'll give them plenty of ammo if you have uncorrected problems.

Third, many home sellers tend to emotionally distance themselves from the home once it's on the market and focus on the next home they're buying. This means that the repairs and upgrades needed to get top dollar get put off and won't happen.

Fourth, a new property on the market usually generates the most interest the first couple of weeks. This is prime time. This is when you'll have the greatest opportunity of attracting a quality buyer.

Time Is Not on the Home Seller's Side

When your home has been on the market for a while with the same ads running week after week and the *For Sale* sign is no longer vertical, the bargain hunter's juices start flowing. Time is not on the side of the seller.

One Realtor who works the bargain hunter niche combs through her local multiple listings looking for homes that have been on the market ninety days or more. These are the ones her clients zero in on and present low offers. They know the sellers are getting discouraged and sometimes downright desperate and often enough will take a low offer to make their problem go away.

Also, according to this agent, the real gold mines are homes that didn't sell for several months, and now the listing has expired. Even if the sellers haven't relisted, chances are the need to sell is still there. They're often discouraged and are wondering what to do next, so they're more likely to jump at a low offer sweetened with a fast closing. Unfortunately, their dreams of getting some equity are replaced by a major pain they want to get rid of so they can get on with their lives.

The longer your home sits on the market the more it costs you. For instance, if you have a 30-year, $150,000, 5.75 percent loan, your daily interest bill is $23.96, or $718 a month. That's money going to the bank's shareholders and not your checking account! And the only way you can stop the negative cash flow is find a buyer ASAP. So you need to make necessary improvements before putting the house on the market to attract buyers quickly.

In Lieu of Fixing Up, How About Carpet and Paint Allowances?

Many sellers try to duck the work of getting their home in prime selling condition by offering a painting and/or upgrade allowance. They rationalize that buyers will jump at the chance to pick out the colors and carpet they want. Unfortunately, this tactic usually backfires and the seller ends up with a low offer in addition to paying the allowance.

The three biggest disadvantages of giving an allowance are:

1. As previously discussed, the buyers who pay top dollar are searching for their dream home. They're buying on emotion, and if your home's condition doesn't fit that dream, they'll move on to the next home.

2. It's difficult to get buyers to visualize what a room would look like if it didn't have 1970s paneling or 1980s wallpaper. Or what new light beige carpet would do for a room with worn-out red shag. It's usually easier for them to look for another home.

Also, Realtors often find it easier to sell their clients a home ready to move into. Trying to get buyers to see the potential in a home and pin down the costs to fix it up is a big pain that most agents are happy to avoid.

3. You give up any negotiating room you may have. Buyers will certainly come in with a low offer and hold your feet to the fire over the allowance too. When you offer a concession up-front, you end up playing defense on their turf, and all you can do is counter with a higher price.

Before moving on to Chapter 3 and showing that first excited couple through your home, scan this last-minute checklist to make sure you're good to go.

☐ Curb appeal (lawns mowed and front yard uncluttered). Inviting to anyone driving by.

☐ Shrubs trimmed and flower beds tidy with colorful annuals (in season).

☐ Walkway to front entry free of clutter and freshly painted.

☐ Entry door, hardware, and doorbell in good condition.

☐ Inside entryway free of clutter and freshly painted.

☐ Kitchen counters clean, magnets and original art work removed from the refrigerator door, and all other rooms clean and decluttered.

☐ Bedrooms in good shape, and closets cleaned and empty.

☐ Bathrooms clean, with fixtures and mirrors sparkling. Tile and caulking around the tub or shower in good condition.

☐ Backyard uncluttered and lawns mowed.

☐ A short break to ask yourself if you're having fun yet.

CHAPTER 3

Marketing Your Home

Once your home is in top selling form, the next step is finding buyers who find your home so attractive that they can't live without it. Price becomes secondary and they wouldn't dare give you a lowball offer for fear of losing it.

This chapter shows you how to go about attracting those types of buyers. This is where rubber meets asphalt. This is where second-best effort won't get you kicked off the island, but it can cost you big bucks and prevent your house from selling quickly.

Different Kinds of Buyers

Broadly speaking there are three types of home buyers. The first are those who are looking for their dream home and when they find it they tend to go with full or close-to-full price offers. These are buyers you want to attract if you want to get the most money possible.

The second type are buyers who want a nice home, but they also want a good deal and tend to bargain shop. They rarely present full-price offers, but go in with low offers and want concessions. Many bargain shoppers look for homes that have been on the market for a while or need some work that they can leverage into a good deal. With this type of buyer you can plan on making counter offers. Sometimes, they'll take your counter if they like your home and feel they're getting a good deal.

This type of buyer can also be a borderline dream home buyer. They may find a home they love, but have the emotional control to try a low offer just to see what happens. If you counter back a bit lower then your asking price, they'll often grab it—satisfied in their mind that they got a good deal.

A good example of this type of buyer is Danny and Luanne, who received an offer from a young couple looking for their first home. When the buyers first walked through they commented on how this was the best home they had looked at. That it was exactly what they were looking for. From their enthusiasm and comments, the sellers knew the buyers really wanted the home.

Later on that day the buyer's agent presented an offer that was $4,500 lower than the asking price. The listing agent, knowing how bad the buyers wanted the home, suggested countering back at $500 less than the asking price. She knew that by letting the buyers "win" something, it would be easier for them to accept the counter—they could tell their friends and family they hadn't paid full price. This scenario happens quite often, and it's worth giving up $500 or $1,000 for a done deal, especially if the buyers are well qualified and ready to go.

The third type of buyers are the hardcore bargain hunters and investors. They're looking for good deals, period. The house is almost secondary. They look for homes that need work or have been on the market for a long time, and for owners who may be distressed. One tactic they often use is to present low offers on numerous houses, an if-you-throw-enough-mud-against-the-wall-some-will-stick approach.

After you've done everything you can to improve your home's condition, the next step in getting high rather than low offers is pricing your home at market value. Price will be one of the first things buyers consider when looking at an ad or visiting your home. You want the price to be at the top of the market, but not over it. Too high and your home doesn't sell; too low and you lose money. You want it just right, and how to do that is the next section.

Getting the Most Money in the Shortest Time

Jim and Rhonda found out the importance of pricing when they tried to sell their home for a year with little success. They even listed with an area broker for six months. Dozens of buyers paraded through their home, mumbled a pleasant "thank you," and drove off.

Obviously, something was wrong. Assuming local economic conditions aren't depressing the housing market, the usual reasons a home doesn't sell are price, location, or condition. In Jim and Rhonda's case, their home's condition and location were comparable with similar homes that were selling in thirty to sixty days. That obviously left price as the culprit.

When asked how they came up with a selling price, these sellers explained that they wanted to move to a more expensive home. In order to do that, they would need to get X number of dollars out of their home. Interestingly, what similar homes were selling for in the area didn't appear to concern them. They hoped if they hung in there, sooner or later a dumb buyer or the tooth fairy would come along and write them a check.

Obviously this approach doesn't work too well, but there are techniques that do and they are discussed next.

Three Easy Steps to Determine the Best Sales Price

To many sellers, pricing their home is like swimming in shark-infested waters while listening to the theme song from *Jaws* on their MP3 player. In reality, it's not too difficult if you stay objective.

Every day thousands of home sellers across the country say to an agent or their spouse something like this: "The Smiths down the block got $250,000 and their home's a dump, so ours has got to be worth at least $295,000." Sorry, but in real life it doesn't work that way and here's why.

To zero in on a price that will get you the most money in the shortest time, you'll need to look at three things: One, what homes similar to yours have sold for in the last three to six months; two, what similar homes are currently selling for in your area; and three, what the competition is in your marketing area for your price range.

Step One: Look at Comparable Sold Properties

In the last chapter it was suggested that you look at similar properties to yours that sold in the last three to six months to find out how your home physically compares. Now you'll want to look at those same comparables but zero in on the following sales data:

1. What were the list prices and the sales prices?

2. Were there any seller concessions, such as paying the buyer's closing costs?

3. How long did it take for the home to sell, or DOM (days-on-market)?

If you haven't got this data, the easiest way is ask a Realtor to look at your home and give you a printout of comparable homes that have sold from the multiple listing system (MLS).

When you look at the comparable homes sold, make sure the age, square footage, style, and neighborhoods are all similar to your home so you're comparing apples to apples. Sometimes inexperienced agents won't make these distinctions and that can skew the results.

For example, if similar homes in your area have sold for $173,500 to $179,700 then you've got a starting point to determine what your home will sell for. However, be aware that you may have to factor in market changes if values are going up or down.

Step Two: Check the Competition's Value

You can also use the homework you did for getting your home ready to sell. Here again, you're looking at the homes on the market competing with yours. In this case you'll zero in on how many homes have sold and how long they have been on the market.

For instance, say that twenty homes have sold in the last thirty days and there are only six homes now on the market. This tells you there's a brisk demand for your price range, and you can price on the high end.

Also, if the market is hot and homes are selling in weeks or days, you'll want to price on the high side. If the home doesn't sell in a few days, you can reduce the price and no harm done.

When homes are selling in days or even hours it's hard to tell how high you can go. In these cases it's best to price a little on the ridiculous side and ratchet down until you get a hit. It's kind of like fly-fishing. You start off with a large attractor fly and then scale down until you get a strike.

A slow market, however, doesn't give you much room to play with pricing. It's important to get it right the first time. So, you'll want to price your home right on what comparable homes are selling for in your area.

Step Three: Position Your Home in the Market

The last but important step is find out where your home fits in the local real estate market. You need to know how many homes in your price range you're competing against.

To illustrate, suppose you've determined that $189,900 is a good price for your home based on similar sold and active properties in your neighborhood. In reality, $189,900 buyers will be looking in other neighborhoods too. So, the next step is to determine what your marketing area is. In other words, if a buyer was looking for a home in your price range, where would they be looking? In some areas it may be county wide, in others several square blocks. Or in the case of condos or co-ops it could even be one building.

A good Realtor will have the experience to know what areas are going to be your competition. For example, when Antonio and Marie put their $298,000 home on the market, their agent told them their likely marketing area would be Kaysville, East Layton, and Farmington. She printed a list of all the $290,000 to $310,000 homes for sale in these adjacent towns. Fortunately, only sixteen homes came up on the search.

The sellers and their agent compared their home's features—such as square footage, age, lot size, bedrooms, baths, and so on—to the others on the list. They found their home was a slightly better buy than nine homes on the list, but the other seven were slightly better in location and finished square footage. Figure 3-1 gives you a list of features that often affect price.

In a normal market, if your home is in the middle of the pack you're priced right on. However, if you're in a slow market where homes are selling in sixty days or more, positioning your home in the bottom 10 to 20 percent may be necessary. Conversely, in a hot market where homes are selling in weeks or days, the strategy would be to price your home in the upper 10 percent.

With this approach, you eliminate a lot of the guesswork and know exactly where you stand relative to the competition. In Antonio and Marie's case, four homes on the list sold before they got an offer. However, if ten or more homes on the list had sold first, then the sellers and agent would need to look closely at price and/or condition and make some adjustments.

Most sellers are emotionally involved with their homes; their egos are often intertwined with their decorating and good taste. They can't understand why any discerning buyer would pick another home over theirs in the same area.

Agents too often add to the problem by not leveling with the sellers, not doing their homework, and not presenting the facts in a clear and concise way. These agents don't want to jeopardize their listing. They're reluctant to rock the boat and alienate the sellers, so they hope for the best and go with the flow even if it means marketing an over-

FIGURE 3-1
Features that commonly influence price.

Feature	Relative Influence
Square Footage	This is a big one. Buyers often compare homes based on square footage and equate this to value.
Age	Also important. It's difficult to compete against homes built in the late 1990s if your home was built in 1983. When doing comparisons, keep year built within five years if possible.
Lot Size	How the house sits on the lot can be important. Usually a .15-acre lot won't compare with a .30-acre lot if buyers in your area want bigger lots. Keep your comparables within .05 acres if possible.
Number of Bedrooms	Depending on the area, 3 bedrooms on one floor are better than 2. But, total bedrooms can be a factor for buyers with kids. Buyers with an elderly family member tend to prefer having a bedroom on the main floor.
Baths	A full bath or shower off the master bedroom is a big plus and brings a better price than a home without. Total baths, like bedrooms, is a factor with families. In comparing homes, the number of baths and where located is important.
Location	This is important to many buyers. A corner lot or a busy street is a negative and should be factored in. Also factor in neighbors, noise, view, and future plans for the area (like a freeway interchange!).
Condition	An oldie but goodie. See Chapter 2.

priced home. Figure 3-2 lists some of the more common pricing mistakes.

The bottom line is it's important to do the homework outlined even if you're planning on using an agent. Thousands of dollars of your money are at stake, so you want to verify that your agent is pricing your home at market value. You'll see why this is critical in the next section.

FIGURE 3-2
Common pricing mistakes and how to correct them.

Sale Killer	Correction
Pricing Your Home Based on What You Feel You Need to Get Out of It	Buyers compare your price to other similar homes for sale in the area. They really don't care what you want. They make offers based on market value. Get an appraisal or look at comparable homes for sale.
Adding the Cost of Improvements and Upgrades to the Home's Value	The value of a home is dependent on other homes in the area. Improvements may help sell the home, but don't necessarily increase the value. Look at similar homes in the area and price accordingly.
Trying to Sell the Home "As Is"	Buyers make good offers on homes they like. If you attract price shoppers and bargain hunters, you'll lose money. Money spent fixing up the home will bring big returns. So tour competitive homes and correct your home's deficiencies with paint, floor coverings, landscaping, and whatever else it needs.
Not Knowing the Competition	Have your agent print out a list of similar homes in the area that are for sale. Go through their open houses or make appointments to see them. Realistically compare the pluses and minuses. Price your home the mid to low end for a faster sale.
Letting Your Ego Get in the Way	Not everyone will agree with your taste no matter how good. And you can't charge extra for your perception of good taste. You may have to redecorate with neutral colors so you appeal to the greatest number of buyers. Look at the competition and do just a little bit better.
Leaving Your Unsold Home on the Market Too Long	If you've overpriced your home or not fixed it up to sell, it can get stale on the market. Take it off and correct the problems. Do your pricing homework and then put it back on the market.
Overpricing Your Home	Most common reasons are overpricing for the location or condition. Obviously, buyers are comparing your home to others and finding your home wanting. You need to do some comparison shopping to get an accurate read on the market. If your home is listed, it's likely agents are using your home to sell others because you're overpriced and make the competition look good.

Don't Make These Mistakes When Working with an Agent

If you're using a Realtor to market your home, most of the legwork tracking down sold and for-sale comparisons will be handled by the agent. However, you don't want to fall into a pricing trap where an unprofessional agent tries to "buy" your listing by inflating the sales price or shortcuts the pricing process.

In fact, this is a trap many sellers fall into when an agent tells them she can sell their home for substantially more than other agents. Greed, denial, and laziness combine to motivate these sellers to go for the long shot. It seldom works out and ends up costing them thousands of dollars.

Alonzo and Marie found this out the hard way when they listed with Marie's cousin, Sherrie, because she was a relative. The sellers didn't question Sherrie's competence nor did they interview any other agents. Although Sherrie was with a large agency, she was new and didn't have much experience or any track record selling homes in the area.

Her pricing strategy was to list the home at the price the sellers wanted to net. The desire to get her clients the most money was good, but pricing a home at what sellers feel they want to walk away with is both naive and unrealistic.

The home went on the market overpriced and languished on the multiple listing for seven long months. Sherrie did the usual marketing with ads, open houses, and putting the home on her office's Wednesday tour day.

By the end of the sixth month, Alonzo and Marie were getting frantic. True, agents showed the home, but nothing happened—not even low offers. What the sellers didn't realize was that other agents were using the home to make other listings look good.

Sometimes agents show overpriced homes first and that makes other homes priced at market value look like bargains. They don't necessarily do this to deceive buyers, but showing homes at market price in contrast to homes that are overpriced is effective marketing.

In Alonzo and Marie's case, it wasn't until they called their agent's broker and requested a meeting were pricing comparables done. When the broker went over the printouts of what similar homes had sold for and what competitive homes were listed for, it became apparent the home was at least $12,000 overpriced.

So how do you find an agent who will level with you on what your home's worth?

What to Look for When You Interview Agents

Finding the best agent for selling your home can be a challenge, but here are five things that will help:

1. Talk to at least three agents. If they all price your home in the same ballpark, that's a good starting point. And if you've done your homework, you know where the ballpark is.

2. Narrow down your short list to those agents who have listed and sold homes in your area and price range. Ask to see copies of sold printouts on homes they've sold. Note the number of days-on-market (DOM) and the list prices and sold prices.

3. When an agent gives you his or her listing presentation, note if the sold and for sale comparisons match up to similar homes in your area, price range, age, square footage, and style. If the comparisons are not close matches, the agent is clueless and doesn't know what's going on. As Donald Trump would then say, "You're fired!"

4. Once you've decided to go with an agent, don't let your ego get in the way. Follow her advice on making your house saleable. She knows the area market and what buyers are looking for.

5. Don't list with a friend or relative unless he's an experienced professional. Friendship and business involving thousands of your dollars rarely mix. You could easily end up losing both.

Even though the data you and your agent used to price your home is accurate, the only opinion that really counts is that of the appraiser. That's because the bank makes a loan based on what the appraiser says the house is worth. As the old saying goes, they who have the gold make the rules. How appraisals work is the next section.

All About Appraisals

Many sellers equate a mortgage lender's or bank's appraisal as an accurate portrayal of their home's value. In reality, this isn't always the case. Appraisers who depend on lenders, builders, and agents for their business will often push the envelope to match an offer or loan amount.

In fact, some mortgage lenders advertise they'll loan up to 120 percent of appraisal. So, it's obvious their appraisers aren't too concerned about getting the numbers right.

The Dark Side of Appraisals

Common examples of pushing the envelope are the Nehemiah and Neighborhood Gold programs, where several thousand dollars are often added to the price to cover the buyer's down payment and closing costs.

If a home is priced at market value and a buyer comes along and needs to go with one of these programs, raising the price is the usual way to handle all or part of the big seller concessions. The appraiser goes along with the inflated price, and the lender makes a loan on a home mortgaged over market value.

Unfortunately, many buyers look only at the low down payment and monthly payments. They don't understand the dark side economics that can result from adding down payments and closing costs to the sales price.

Down the road, if they need to sell, there's no equity when the loan balance exceeds the market value. Many of these homeowners wonder why their home appraised for so much when they bought it, but now isn't worth that price when they want to sell.

Also the mortgage industry is increasingly credit-score driven. Lenders will often approve a higher sales price on a given property for buyers with high credit scores than they will for those with marginal scores. This tends to put buyers in homes that can take years to reach a break-even point before they start building equity.

In one particular case, a home was priced at market value of $190,000. An offer came in at $188,000 with a concession written in that the sellers pay $8,100 of the buyer's costs.

Understandably, the sellers were upset, but they had made an offer on a condo and the buyer had a prequalification letter from his lender verifying he was good to go. The sellers didn't want to lose a sure sale, but they couldn't take a big loss either. By taking the offer they would have lost $10,100— $2,000 from the low offer and $8,100 from paying concessions.

Giving it their best shot, the sellers countered, raising the sale price to $194,000 but offering to pay the $8,100. This reduced their net by $4,100, an amount they could live with.

The end result was that the buyers, who had little money for down payment or closing costs, were able to buy a home. True, the price was inflated, and the sellers were essentially financing the buyers' down payment and closing costs.

Is this ethical? Certainly. The buyers have the right to make their own financial decisions, even though they may have to stay in the home for an extended period before the loan is paid down to the home's market value. In defense, many lenders will say it's better to buy a home now than wait until prices have gone up. It's a judgment call.

Will mortgage lenders make this type of loan? They do it all the time. All they care about is whether the appraisal comes in at the sales price and the buyers qualify. Some lenders even loan up to 120 percent of appraisal depending on the buyer's credit.

This brings us back to the dark side of appraisals. An appraiser can scour the area for homes that have sold a little high and stretch the envelope here or there. Plus, the faraway loan underwriter who approves the loan may have loose appraisal standards or not be savvy on the local market.

Not surprisingly in this case, the appraisal came in at the countered price of $145,990. The buyers were happy because they got into a home for nothing down, and the sellers got their home sold.

The bottom line of all this is appraisals are not an exact science. Although appraisers are supposed to follow industry and government guidelines, sales price, likes and dislikes, and builder and lender pressure all influence the results.

The Type of Loan Can Also Affect the Appraisal

What type of loan a buyer decides to get can affect the appraisal. Basically, there are three loan types: Federal Housing Administration (FHA); Fannie Mae, Freddie Mac, and a host of smaller banks (conventional); and Veterans Affairs guaranteed loans (VA). Each type has its own appraisal standards that can make a difference, namely:

■ *Fannie Mae* and *Freddie Mac (conventional) appraisals* are typically less restrictive and more forgiving of a home's condition than FHA/VA. For example, if you have 20 percent or more down payment, a good credit score in the 700s, and a couple of months' payments in reserve, you may not even need a formal appraisal. If data on the home is available from tax records or a previous sale, the lender may require only a drive-by to verify the home is as represented in the paperwork.

■ *FHA appraisals* are more exacting than conventional loans because their mission is geared more toward first-time home buyers. The appraisers have a detailed five-page checklist they complete, and the house must meet certain condition standards. The government wants to make sure buyers have some protection when they buy a home.

So if your home is older or may need some work done, you could get a list of repair items attached to an FHA appraisal that you wouldn't get with a conventional one. But the trade-off is that in some areas the buyer pool will be considerably larger with an FHA mortgage.

■ *VA appraisals* are similar to FHA in that they require the property to be in reasonably good condition. The VA mission is to look out for veterans and their appraisals will tend to look for problems that conventional appraisals would ignore.

Hopefully you've now got a price for your home nailed down, and have a good idea of what appraisals are all about. Now it's time to have some fun talking to buyers.

How to Use Signs, Brochure Boxes, and Fliers to Attract Buyers

When you list your home with a Realtor, they'll install yard signs and directional signs to funnel people to your property, and they'll provide brochure boxes and fliers. If they don't have a flier box, you'll need to apply a little pressure to get one installed ASAP along with a good supply of fliers. Better still, make sure the agent you choose to list your home with agrees to do this before you sign up.

This is important, because the first few hours after a sign is planted are critical. Neighbors and people driving by will notice the sign and, hopefully, grab a flier while their interest is high. Many homes sell quickly when a neighbor passes a flier along to a friend or relative who wants to live in the area.

For this reason, you may want to make sure your agent passes out fliers to homeowners on your block and nearby streets as soon as possible after the sign goes up.

Sign Savvy for "Fizzbos" (For Sale by Owners)

If you decide to try and sell your home on your own for a few weeks, you'll first need to plant a *For Sale* sign or two. It doesn't have to be elaborate, high-tech, or overly big—18 inches by 24 inches with space to write in a phone number is big enough. The plastic red and white *For Sale* signs found in hardware stores, Walmart, K-Mart, and similar stores are perfect. Signs are cheap, effective, and along with fliers give you the most marketing bang for the buck.

Write your phone number on the sign in letters big and dark

enough to be read from the street. Don't try to put the price, number of bedrooms, baths, or other info on the sign—just one large phone number that people driving by can read at a glance. Keep it simple; the home's features, amenities, and price go on the flier.

Use your cell phone number if you have one, otherwise go with your home phone. However, keep in mind that if you put your home number on the sign and use an answering machine to pick up when you're not there, you may miss calls and a possible sale. For some reason, drive-bys don't like to leave messages.

Interestingly, people will park in front of your house or close by and call you from their cell phone. Callers are impatient. They want details and want them now while the iron is hot. If they get an answering machine, you'll likely never hear from them again.

In addition to the yard sign (two if you're on a corner), directional signs on nearby intersections can funnel lookers to your house. However, before you install any signs check with city hall. They may have ordinances against signs on corners and intersections. Also check with your homeowners' association if you have one. Sometimes they get uptight about any *For Sale* signs, including the one on your lawn.

Fliers and Brochure Boxes

Attaching a flier box to your sign can be a great marketing tool. It tells drive-bys all about your home 24 hours a day 7 days a week. An informative flier can turn a lukewarm prospect into a hot buyer. So, you'll definitely want to install a box and keep it well supplied.

You can order flier boxes through the Internet at:

www.myboardstore.com

www.victorystore.com

www.plasticfab.com

www.realtysignexpress.com

www.homesbyowner.com

To be effective, your flier doesn't need to be an elaborate four-color job. A "just the facts" bulleted list works great. Facts you'll want to include are:

- Price. Always put the price on your flier. It cuts down on unnecessary calls from people looking in different price ranges. Realtors sometimes leave off prices in their ads and fliers to encourage calls, but they're looking to pick up clients for all price ranges.

- Square footage for each level, and the total. This is livable footage. Garage and unlivable basement space shouldn't be included. But, if you have a full unfinished basement with seven-

or eight-foot ceilings, windows, and it complies with local building codes for finishing, be sure to note that on your flier.

■ Number of bedrooms on each level, including the size of the master bedroom and whether you have single, double, or walk-in closets.

■ Number of baths on each level. Indicate whether they are full (tub/shower), 3/4 (shower only), or 1/2 baths (toilet and sink only). Also include details such as jetted tub, tub/shower combo, and walk-in closets.

■ Kitchens are important, so list appliances and unusual amenities. For example, items such as a Viking gas range, extra large pantry, super-quiet dishwasher, or island with sink or range should be highlighted.

■ The age and type of roof.

■ Year built and/or year remodeled.

■ School district and the addresses of the schools.

■ Any other amenities unique to and desirable in your neighborhood.

Some sellers put a lot of effort into professional-looking fliers with color interior and exterior images. They look nice, but unfortunately seldom result in more appointments or a quicker sale.

A sample flier is shown in Figure 3-3.

Finally, keep track of the number of fliers you put in the box so you can tell how many people are stopping by. It's not unusual to go through a few dozen fliers the first week or two. After all, the neighbors have to see what you're asking.

It's important to remember that the mission of your sign and flier is to simply get the phone to ring. The callers have seen the outside of your home and the flier's job is to kick the interest level up a notch or two so they'll call you. Too much information on the sheet can sometimes hurt if it causes a buyer to prejudge the home and not call you.

Getting Mortgage Companies to Help with Fliers

In some areas mortgage lenders offer to print fliers, lend you *For Sale* signs, and help with paperwork if you'll let them plant their sign alongside yours. These loan officers hope they can snag a buyer who likes your home but hasn't got a lender. This can be a good deal for you.

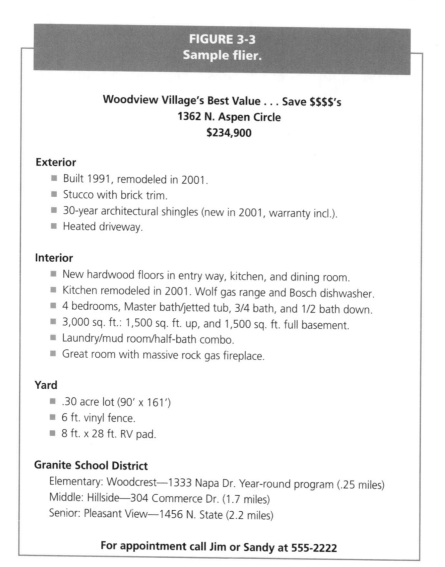

FIGURE 3-3
Sample flier.

Woodview Village's Best Value . . . Save $$$$'s
1362 N. Aspen Circle
$234,900

Exterior
- Built 1991, remodeled in 2001.
- Stucco with brick trim.
- 30-year architectural shingles (new in 2001, warranty incl.).
- Heated driveway.

Interior
- New hardwood floors in entry way, kitchen, and dining room.
- Kitchen remodeled in 2001. Wolf gas range and Bosch dishwasher.
- 4 bedrooms, Master bath/jetted tub, 3/4 bath, and 1/2 bath down.
- 3,000 sq. ft.: 1,500 sq. ft. up, and 1,500 sq. ft. full basement.
- Laundry/mud room/half-bath combo.
- Great room with massive rock gas fireplace.

Yard
- .30 acre lot (90' x 161')
- 6 ft. vinyl fence.
- 8 ft. x 28 ft. RV pad.

Granite School District
Elementary: Woodcrest—1333 Napa Dr. Year-round program (.25 miles)
Middle: Hillside—304 Commerce Dr. (1.7 miles)
Senior: Pleasant View—1456 N. State (2.2 miles)

For appointment call Jim or Sandy at 555-2222

After all, you've got nothing to lose. Why not go for all the free help you can get?

Plus, if you get an interested party and they're not prequalified, you can refer them to this lender and quickly find out if you have a good prospect or a deadbeat.

In the event no lenders call from your ads, you'll need to get proactive and call around. Some ways to find a good lender who does this are:

■ If your mortgage company has a local office, give them a call and ask for their best loan officer.

■ Talk to Realtors or title people, they know who the best loan officers are.

■ Ask friends and relatives who have bought homes recently whom they used.

■ Check out lenders who are advertising in your local paper.

■ Go to the Mortgage Bankers Association Web site, *www.mbaa .org,* and click on links to state and local sites.

Once you find a good lender, invite her to put up a sign and work with you in selling your home, and you'll refer any prospects that come through.

Along with signs and brochures, ads are the workhorses of selling homes. How to write effective, house-selling ads is next.

How to Write Killer Ads

As with yard signs and fliers, if you go with an agent you won't have to worry too much about ads. But, if you decide to give it a try on your own for a while, effective ads will be an important part of your marketing plan.

Some tips in writing effective, four-line ads are:

1. Don't include words like desperate, must sell, price reduced, make offer, motivated seller, moving, and so on. You want to attract people who are looking for their dream home, not bargain hunters who zero in on distressed properties.

2. Ask yourself what's the most desirable feature about your home; what attracted you enough to make an offer? Once you've decided on that feature, it becomes your headline. For example, if the best feature is schools—and buyers do look for homes in certain school boundaries—a headline could feature the school district. For example:

Northcross School District
1998 ranch, 3 bdrm, 2.5 baths,
2,800 sq. ft., .30 acre lot.
$288,000, 801-555-1234.

If the biggest feature is the view or lot size, headlines could read: *One-Half Acre Wooded Lot,* or *Panoramic View of Beaver Lake,* or *Awesome Ocean View*

Another effective headline can be your address, if your home is in a desirable area that sells quickly. Many home buyers tend to skim the classifieds looking for homes in specific neighborhoods, and the following sample ad emphasizes the address:

1374 Woodland Hills Dr.
$376,000, remodeled 1978 tudor,
3,200 sq.ft., 4 bdrms, 3 baths,
.50 acre lot, 801-555-2323.

It is important to include the price so you can eliminate those who are looking in a different price range. Realtors often leave the price out to encourage calls. You, on the other hand, want to get only calls from buyers in your price range.

3. Run your ads on Saturdays and Sundays when serious home buyers are most likely to have the time to scout out neighborhoods they're interested in.

4. Ads in large metro dailies tend to get lost in a sea of four liners. It's often more effective and cheaper to run your ad in local weeklies and community papers. Also, shelf life of the weekly papers is usually longer than the bigger dailies.

5. Advertising in "homes for sale" magazines can be effective. There are even publications devoted to FSBO ads only. Check newspaper racks at supermarkets, convenience stores, and gas stations for what's available in your area.

One advantage of advertising in the "homes for sale" magazines is you'll be able to run a photo or two of your home. If, unlike your driver's license or passport photo—your home is photogenic, great photos can generate a lot of quality calls.

Cost-wise, the ads are reasonable and shelf life is two weeks to thirty days. Additionally, some of these magazines are na-

> **Check what magazines are available in your area. Three national publications worth checking out are:**
> *www.forsalebyowner.com*
> *www.harmonhomes.com*
> *www.usahomes.org*

tional, and out-of-state buyers can view properties over the Internet or order copies.

With your signs up, brochure box stuffed full of fliers, and ads in your local weekly, the phone is going to ring. How to handle all these calls effectively is next.

How to Handle Ad Calls and Showings

The phone is ringing. People want to know all about the house. Where do you start? Do you tell them to come on by? Here are some suggestions to make the situation more manageable. First, you'll want to go with appointments only. This is important not only because of security, but it's almost impossible to keep the house in showing condition all the time—especially if you have kids and a black lab retriever.

Undoubtedly, you'll have your share of people who call from the curb on their cell phone wanting to see the home. If it's convenient, go for it. If not, schedule a time that works for both of you. If the caller refuses to set up an appointment and roars off, don't worry about it. Serious buyers understand and will gladly set up a time to come back.

Second, keep a log of the people who call you. You may have to call them back if a problem comes up and you need to reschedule. Also, people who know you have their name and phone number are more likely to take the appointment seriously and show up.

Third, depending on the price range and the type of calls you're getting, you may find it necessary to screen your appointments to cut down on the lookers and tire kickers.

For instance, you may ask callers if they've talked to a lender and are prequalified for $475,000 or whatever. Some sellers find this controversial, and feel it may offend potential buyers.

However, many sellers using this approach have found that serious buyers are seldom offended. In fact, they appreciate your candor and respect your efforts to cut down on lookers. Tire kickers, on the other hand, will probably just hang up on you.

Before You Show Your Home

Security is an important part of selling your home. Horror stories frequently appear in newspapers about homeowners and Realtors being attacked while showing homes. A few precautions up front can help prevent serious problems. Consider these suggestions to make your showings safer:

- Show your home by appointment only and get names and phone numbers.

- Jot down car license numbers of people who come through.

- Don't leave any valuables in sight or in easy-to-find places like drawers or closets.

- Don't leave prescription drugs in cabinets or drawers.

- If you have valuable collections, antiques, art work, etc., seriously consider renting a secure storage unit.

- Never show the home when you're alone. Arrange for a neighbor or friend to come over during appointments if you're going to be the only one home.

- Never schedule an appointment after dark. Not only for security reasons, but buyers are unlikely to make an offer on a home where they can't see the roof, exterior, or yard.

One advantage of working with an agent is that buyers are usually pre-screened and the agent escorts them through your home. Even then, you should still follow the suggestions above. Agents have no way of knowing if their clients are sticky fingered or serial killers.

A favorite tactic of the bad guys in showings and open houses is for several people to come through the home together. While one or two distract the homeowner or the agent, the others can clean out any easy-to-carry valuables and prescriptions they can find.

Showing Your House When Listed with an Agent

When you list your home, showing appointments will either be handled through your Realtor, or cooperating agents on the MLS can call you directly. Local MLS rules and company policies can differ from area to area.

If MLS rules permit, you'll likely get calls from agents who see your sign while showing homes in the area. They may even call you from the curb asking if they can show it immediately.

In these cases, it's likely the agent has prequalified the buyers before taking them out and may have missed your home when putting a list together. Still, like any other call from the curb, if it's inconvenient you should offer to set up a time. If the buyers are interested, they'll gladly come back.

Normally, agents bringing their clients through will have a printout of your home's features. But for situations where agents call you from the curb, it's a good idea to have your Realtor give you a supply of fliers to pass out.

Also, when an agent shows the home, it's usually best to take the dog for a walk or run a few errands so you're not in the way. Agents like the owners to disappear so their buyers can relax and talk about what they like and dislike about the home without offending anyone.

Showing Your Home When Selling by Owner

Hopefully by the time your appointment rings the doorbell, the impressions formed from walking up to the front door are positive. They should be ringing your doorbell with mounting anticipation, eager to see what could be their dream home.

You're probably experiencing stomach butterflies and anxiety hoping the buyers will like your home, that they won't make a U-turn in the entryway and leave without going through the home.

In reality, it goes smoothly. Welcome the buyers in, give them a flier, and let them walk through the home. If they have questions, you'll be available in the kitchen or family room.

It's best not to shadow prospective buyers from room to room with a nonstop dialogue of the home's features. Let them talk about what they like and don't like among themselves without hovering nearby.

You want buyers to relax and zero in on what's important to them so they can visualize their possessions in the rooms and how they would decorate. If they like what they see and are interested in going further, they'll let you know by asking questions about price, how much time you need to move, and what appliances you're including.

Specifics on negotiating and writing offers are covered in Chapter 4, Handling Offers: The Art of the Deal.

So you don't get discouraged, it's important to remember that not everyone has the same taste. Even if you've decorated in neutral colors and the home looks terrific, you may still get a few people who don't like your home. Some buyers even bad mouth a home they like hoping to camouflage their interest or soften up the sellers for a possible offer.

So, take comments from lookers with a grain of salt. Often people who gush over your home and decorating and tell you how perfect it is, walk out the door never to return. As the saying goes, you sift through the chaff to find the golden kernel.

The next marketing tool is how to hold an effective open house that may attract that golden buyer.

What About Open Houses?

Realtors hold open houses not only to sell your home but to find new clients as well. They know from experience that most lookers either have a house to sell before they buy or qualify for a different price range.

On the other hand, your sole purpose is to sell your home. If it's in a desirable area and people are cruising the boulevards looking, your chances of snagging a buyer are good. Enough homes sell through open houses to seriously consider having them.

Be aware though that open houses can also be frustrating. You can attract a stream of tire kickers, curious neighbors, and people who make a hobby of going to open houses. Just remember, it's like panning for gold. You're looking for a shiny nugget buried in the stream bottom. If you swirl enough gravel and water in the pan, eventually you'll catch the gleam of pure gold. It's a matter of patience and hanging in there.

If you're working with an agent, all you have to do is make sure the house is clean and find somewhere to go for a few hours; the agent does the rest. However, if you're going the FSBO route, here are a few tips on holding a successful open house:

- Put together a flier or add the date and time of your open house to your existing one. Pass these around the area three to five days before the open house.

- Plant as many directional signs (ones with an arrow) as needed to funnel traffic to your street.

- Buy some multicolored flags on long streamers and run them from the roof to a fence or ground stake. You want lookers to be able to spot your home instantly when they turn onto your street. Look in the yellow pages under advertising specialties for 30-, 50-, and 100-foot streamers.

- Place an ad in your local daily so it appears the morning of the open house. Be sure the price and address are in the ad.

- When people come to the door, give them a flier and tell them they're free to wander around. If they have any questions you'll be in the family room.

- Don't set up your command center in the kitchen, because this is where most people go first. Fewer people and less clutter in the kitchen make it appear larger.

■ Have a mortgage lender lined up whom you can call if a looker turns into a serious prospect. Also, don't sign a sales contract until you've made sure the buyer is prequalified and good to go. That means you'll need to call their mortgage lender if they have one and verify they've got their financial ducks lined up.

The checklist below is a useful summary of all you need to do to market your home successfully.

☐ You've checked what similar homes have sold for, what's now on the market competing with you, and set your price to be competitive.

☐ Home and curb appeal in top showing condition.

☐ For sale and directional signs planted. Phone number on the sign big enough so you can read it from the street.

☐ Fifty to a hundred fliers printed.

☐ Brochure box planted with twenty-five fliers to start.

☐ Ads written and called in for the weekend.

☐ A minimum of thirty fliers about the open house passed around the neighborhood.

☐ Mortgage lender contacted with their sign installed.

☐ Two copies of your state's approved real estate purchase contract.

☐ A string of colored flags for the open house if you plan one for the weekend.

☐ Open house date and time printed on your flier and passed around three to five days before the event.

☐ Fliers taken along wherever you go and passed out at work, in area businesses, at the hair stylist. Be creative, the more fliers floating around the better.

☐ Security precautions taken. Never set up appointments after dark and when you're alone. If needed, arrange to have a friend come over when showing the house. Get names and phone numbers. If possible jot down car license numbers.

Tips for Marketing Your Home in Extreme Markets

The real estate market is in constant motion. Like a giant pendulum it swings from a buyer's market to a seller's market and back again.

Where the market is in the arc depends on many factors. The most common factors are interest rates and what direction they're heading, local employment, and the national economy. These factors in turn affect the number of homes on the market.

Buyer's Market (Polar Bear Country)

A buyer's market is created when there are more homes on the market than buyers. In a slow market, people still buy homes, but the properties in less desirable locations suffer first.

You can look at it as a pyramid (see Figure 3-4). The greatest number of homes in less desirable locations are at the bottom. As you move up the pyramid, the location and homes improve, but there are also fewer for sale. The upper 10 to 20 percent are homes in good areas that will sell quickly and for close to or full price.

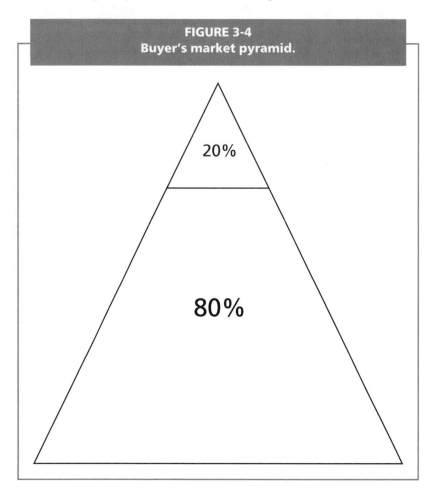

FIGURE 3-4
Buyer's market pyramid.

20%

80%

The bottom 80 percent will lose value and take longer to sell. As a buyer's market worsens, the difficulty in selling a home climbs up the pyramid, but rarely reaches the upper 10 percent.

It's important to note that the upper part of the pyramid is not always the most expensive homes. In every area there are high-demand neighborhoods that are close to great schools, medical centers, office buildings, or some other desirable location. In fact, in some buyer's markets the most expensive homes nosedive first, lose a bigger percentage of their equity, and recover last.

The middle part of the pyramid can also take a big hit in a down market. Entry-level homeowners near the bottom sell and move up to the mid-priced homes. But if they can't sell, they can't move up to the middle layer, and then that layer can't move up or buy new construction.

High interest rates, recession, a local employer shutting down or cutting back on its workforce—these are some causes of a buyer's market. In fact, anything that affects the local housing market negatively or seasonally can cause a short- or long-term buyer's market.

In this type of market, prices and terms soften, and to sell you may need to pay buyer concessions. Typical concessions that can make you more competitive are:

■ Pay all or part of the buyer's closing costs. This will typically be 2.5 to 3 percent of the loan amount. On a $165,000 home that would cost you $4,125 to $4,950. Sometimes you can raise the price to compensate for part of this cost, but that would depend on market conditions and how serious the buyers are.

■ You can pay points to help the buyers qualify for the loan. Points are interest you pay on behalf of the borrower to lower their interest rate. Each point equals 1 percent of the loan amount and lowers the interest rate about one-fifth of a percent. See Chapter 6 for a discussion of points and how to use them as a sale tool.

■ You may tip the sale in your favor by throwing in appliances, such as the refrigerator, washer and dryer, furniture, or, as one seller did, a big screen TV.

Installing new carpeting and/or painting can work. But, don't offer it unless you need it to close the deal. Throw in an allowance up front and you'll lose a strong bargaining chip.

Of course, you can always drop the price. However, for many sellers that may not be an option, as Mark and Rachael found out when

Mark's employer consolidated branches and moved his office to another town. That left Mark and Rachael with two choices: either sell and relocate or find a new job in an economically down area. They decided to accept the relocation and sell their three-year-old home.

Because they had recently refinanced their mortgage and paid off a few credit cards, Mark and Rachael had little equity left. They had no room to pay concessions or lower their asking price. They were in a financial corner with few options that wouldn't cost them thousands of dollars in the months ahead. In the end they had to rent their home to cover as much of the mortgage payment as possible. Eventually, they hoped the market would improve so they could sell the home for what they owed.

A slow market is where listing with a Realtor can be the best move. They have the multiple listing service on their side and attract a high percentage of the qualified buyers. Most agents also have the expertise to put difficult deals together that become common in a slow market.

In one particular case, a couple was transferred and couldn't rent out their home because of mortgage restrictions. They had little equity and few options. However, they did find a local broker who agreed to list their home for a reduced commission. After about two months on the market, the broker found a buyer, but to make the deal work, the sellers would have to pay $2,700 of the buyer's closing fees.

After doing the math, the sellers decided to accept the offer. It meant they would have to pay $2,700 at closing but they would eliminate the $900-a-month loan payments and they would no longer have to worry about leaving the house vacant.

In a slow market you sometimes have to weigh the options and go with the one less painful in the long run.

The Thrill of a Seller's Market

On the flip side, a seller's market is the result of there being more buyers than homes for sale. Since real estate is a function of supply and demand, fewer homes on the market create a rising tide where all home values in the area go up. The more desirable areas, however, go up faster and top out higher before the market flattens out. The truism, location is everything, becomes obvious in this situation.

Also when home prices are going up dramatically, entry- and mid-level homes become especially hard to find. Since condos and townhouses are less expensive to get into and tend to attract first-time home buyers, this market can explode.

Homeowners who bought when the market pendulum was in buyer's territory will see their return on investment skyrocket. If you've outgrown your condo or townhouse, this would be the time to cash out and move up.

Tips for Getting the Most Money in a Seller's Market

- Realtors are going to hate this, but you don't need to pay 6 or 7 percent in a sizzling market. A *For Sale* sign and ad are most likely all you need if your home is in good condition and priced reasonably.

- Line up an attorney or someone who can help with the sales forms when you get a hot buyer. Likewise, have a lender lined up in case you need to refer a buyer.

- In a hot market, you can afford to be picky, so ask any caller if they've talked to a lender and are prequalified for your sales price. There's no reason to show anyone through who is merely looking and not a qualified buyer.

- It's likely you'll get more than one offer at the same time. In hot markets, buyers sometimes have to go 5, 10, or 20 percent over asking price to even be in the game. For tips on how to handle multiple offers check out Chapter 4, Handling Offers: The Art of the Deal.

Now that you've got your marketing project in full swing, the next chapter shows how to deal with the buyers your marketing attracts so you'll net the most money possible.

Handling Offers:
The Art of the Deal

Now that your marketing program is underway and people are going through your home, it shouldn't take too long before you get an offer. This chapter shows you how to handle different types of offers and presents a few to-do lists to help make the transaction go smoothly.

What's a Binding Offer?

To make sure that everyone's on the same page, an offer is defined as follows: *A filled out and signed real estate sales agreement with adden-dums using your state's approved forms and an earnest money check attached.*

Anything less is what powers the big colorful balloons you see at fairs and carnivals.

Why is this so important? Because in every state a valid and enforceable real estate contract must be in writing, signed by both parties, along with valuable consideration. Normally the consideration is a personal or cashier's check, but it can be a promissory note or anything of value that both parties agree to.

Addendum Savvy

A form equally important to the purchase contract and making a deal work is the addendum. It's a form that's used to write additional terms, conditions, concessions, or anything not contained in the real estate purchase contract. They can be written on a formal multipart form, a letterhead, or a blank piece of paper.

Typically, these forms contain a reference to the purchase contract, date, buyer and seller, property address, and a deadline for the buyer or seller to respond. The rest is the addendum.

Both buyers and sellers must sign and date the addendum for it to be binding on the deal.

Typical uses of addendums in the sales process are:

■ To remove financing, appraisal, and other contingencies contained in the purchase agreement so they are no longer part of the deal. For example, you would remove the loan approval condition with an addendum that states the deal is no longer subject to buyers' qualifying for financing.

■ If you're buying a new home the builder will often use addendums for change orders, extensions, signing off on deadlines, and so on.

■ If the deal is subject to a home inspection, the buyers can come back with an addendum requiring certain items be upgraded or repaired. You can accept and sign it. Or you can counter with a new addendum labeled "Counter Addendum X," and write in your counter terms along with a deadline for response.

■ Addendum forms are used for countering an offer and listing those items you will do. As mentioned, always put a time limit for the buyers to respond so you're not tied up if a new offer comes in.

■ All addendums should be numbered in the order they happen and the pages should be numbered 1/x, 2/x, and so on, with x being the number of pages.

For example, an offer may have an FHA financing addendum, #1; a lead-based paint addendum, #2; and an addendum containing a

Sources of real estate forms if you're going FSBO
Ask a friendly real estate agent for a set of sales forms. Agents are usually cooperative because they know you'll be calling them if you can't sell on your own.

Use a search engine such as Google, then key in [your state], and then "real estate forms." Or check out the following Web sites:
www.urgentbusinessforms.com
www.uslegalforms.com
www.1stoplegal.com

buyer concession, #3. And if you were to counter the offer, that would be #4.

If you're going FSBO, it's important for you to have a working knowledge of your state's real estate forms and how to fill them out. It's also a good idea to have a Realtor or attorney explain them to you and line up help if needed when an offer comes in.

It can't be emphasized too strongly that accurate paperwork is a must. You'll need to make sure the forms are complete and clear for everyone involved. Mistakes cost you money; big mistakes cost you a lot of money.

This is not to scare you, but to point out that if you want your closing check as soon as possible, filling out the paperwork correctly and keeping track of the various deadlines are critical.

How to respond to offers is detailed in the next few sections.

What Kind of Offers Can You Expect?

Seasoned or first-time homebuyers looking for their dream home are the people you most want to get offers from. If your home is what they've been looking for, price becomes secondary. True, they may come in with a low offer, but when you counter back at your lowest price, they'll most often take it. They don't want to lose the house anymore than you want to lose a buyer. But, they've got to try and get it for less. It's the American way. After all, what are they going to tell their friends or their mom and dad who told them to never pay full price for anything—unless they really want it.

Sometimes you have to play the game, and come down a few hundred dollars or throw in an appliance to make the deal work, but it's worth it.

The next category, bargain hunters are like telemarketers: Their calls come at any time and their offers are low.

Low Offers from Bargain Buyers

When the market is hot, you don't see as many low offers . . . unless coming in 10 percent over asking price when everyone else is offering 20 percent is low.

Bargain hunters are looking for a steal. What drives these buyers is price more than the home's condition. They usually do a quick walk through and their questions tend to zero in on why you're selling and if you would take less. If you do get an offer, it'll be way low and when you counter they'll usually move on to their next project.

Bargain buyers especially look for homes that need work they can pick up cheap and improve. If you've put your home in good selling shape, you'll attract fewer of these buyers as well as fewer investors.

Investor Offers

These buyers are most active whenever a real estate guru comes to town with a get-rich-with-real-estate seminar. Naturally, they'll have to buy a property with a huge discount to make their project work. So you want to make sure it isn't your house they zero in on.

Don't get the wrong impression, not all investors are bad. Many are honest business people who buy run-down properties and fix them up to resell. They provide a real service in the community, giving these homes a second life. A family gets a reconditioned home in better shape than they might have otherwise.

If you do have a home that you're thinking of selling to an investor (or any other buyer), here are three pitfalls you'll want to avoid:

1. Never take back a note for part of your equity. If they want to buy your home, make it a cash-out deal. There are currently many financing programs for nonowner-occupied home buyers. If a bank won't finance them because of bad credit, what chance do you stand in collecting a note.

2. Never let a buyer assume your mortgage without qualifying through your lender. Similarly, don't be a party to a wrap-around or an all-inclusive trust deed. You're still on the hook with your mortgage company, and if the buyer misses payments or defaults you're the one they'll come after. Plus, most lenders' trust deeds state that conveying all or part of your ownership can trigger a foreclosure.

Arnie and Jackie fell into this trap when they got transferred to another city a couple of states away. Their loan had a nonassumption clause like most do, but they wanted out so bad they let an investor buy their home with a wrap-around trust deed and left town. A few months later they got a letter from their lender informing them they were calling the loan due for defaulting on the due-on-sale clause in the trust deed.

The investor had problems renting the property and when the lender checked the title because of missed payments, they discovered the recorded wrap-around deed. That triggered the default and, unfortunately, there was nothing Arnie and Jackie could do but watch their credit sink to the bottom for a couple of years.

3. In addition to illegal assumptions, never sell your home on a lease-option or any other creative approach where you don't control the payments. The big majority of these deals fail, and you can easily be left with missed payments, a trashed house, and foreclosure notices.

Now that you have an idea of what kinds of offers you may get, the next step is the fun part, responding to offers.

Offer Basics

Getting an offer on your home is an emotional event. It ranks up there with your first date: a disaster (low-ball offer), so-so (you counter the offer), or you're hopelessly in love (full-price offer).

Whether you're selling FSBO or working with an agent, your typical response to an offer will likely be:

1. It's a great offer, the buyers have their financing lined up, and the closing date is acceptable. You sign the paperwork and the deal is done.

2. It's not quite what you want, so you write what is acceptable on an addendum or counter-offer form and send it back to the buyers. If they sign it, it's a done deal. If not, it can sometimes bounce back and forth until a meeting-of-the-minds happens or the parties walk away.

3. The offer is so far off the mark that you don't want anything to do with these buyers or their offer. You check the rejection box and sign. Hopefully you'll never hear from these time wasters again.

Handling Earnest Money, Closing Dates, and Verifications

When an offer comes in (see the Offer Checklist below), first make sure the buyers have a letter from their lender confirming they're pre-qualified and good to go. Of course, you could call their lender and verify they're approved, but that's a pain. It's better to tell them, when they call for an appointment to bring their offer by, to include a letter from their lender.

Second, ask for as big an earnest-money deposit as you can get. The hotter the market, the bigger deposit you can ask for. Depending on the area, deposits go from $100 to 1 percent or more of the sales price. Ask a Realtor or mortgager lender what is the norm in your market.

Third, go with the shortest possible closing period, because that will mean more money in your pocket due to less interest paid. Most conventional lenders prorate the month's interest from the day the lender receives the payoff in their account.

For instance, if the monthly interest on your loan is $987, dividing that by 30 days gives you the $32.90 you're paying per day in interest. If the lender receives the payoff funds on the 14th, you pay $32.90 × 14, or $460.60. As you can see, the sooner you close the more you save.

However, FHA loans generally don't prorate, so you'll pay an entire month's interest no matter on what day you close. Check with your mortgage lender and verify their prorating policy. It can mean several hundred dollars more in your pocket.

Offer Checklist

☐ Make sure all the purchase contract pages and addendums are dated, signed, or initialed where needed.

☐ Make sure that a letter from the buyer's mortgage lender is attached, verifying they have been approved for at least the sales price.

☐ Get a reasonable earnest money deposit, one that will compensate you for taking the home off the market if the buyers back out.

☐ Note the closing date on the paperwork. Can you live with it?

☐ Have a Realtor or attorney look at the paperwork before you commit.

Deadlines Are Important

Important components of the sales agreement usually come with deadlines for completion by either the buyer or seller. These vary from state to state, but the most common deadlines are:

■ *Amount of Time to Accept, Reject, or Counter the Offer*. This commonly varies from "upon presentation" to 48 hours or more. Also, when you counter an offer you'll write in a deadline for the buyer to respond, usually 12 to 24 hours.

■ *Loan Application and Fee Deadlines*. Hopefully, this is already done and you can write in "completed" if the form has a line for this.

■ *Seller Disclosures.* If your state's form has this line, five days is sufficient for you to fill out these forms and get them to the buyer. It's a good idea to fill these forms out when you put your home on the market so you can give a copy to serious buyers.

■ *Evaluations and Inspections Deadlines.* If a buyer is using a home inspector or other inspectors for radon, mold, termites, survey, and so on, you'll want to have deadlines for their completion. Usually, five to ten days is enough time.

■ *Loan Denial Deadline.* This is an important deadline. If the loan is denied after this date, the buyers could lose their earnest-money deposit. Ten days should be ample time, especially if the buyers are pre-approved.

However, even though a buyer is preapproved, things can happen in the weeks between purchase and closing. In one case, a buyer was terminated on his job the day before closing. Although this was unfortunate, the sellers got to keep the deposit because they had taken their home off the market for three weeks. Check with an attorney or your state's real estate department for what's legal in your area.

■ *Appraisal Deadline.* Ten days should be plenty of time for the lender to get their appraiser through your home.

■ *Settlement or Closing Deadline.* This is when the loan paperwork is completed and everyone goes to the office of the title company, lender, or attorney to sign the documents.

As mentioned above, you want to keep this as tight as possible because the interest clock on your loan is still ticking. Thirty days should be the maximum unless there are good reasons to make it longer.

■ *Possession.* How long you have after everyone signs the paperwork at closing to move out and give the keys to the buyers is an important deadline. This can vary from area to area, but normally two to three days is enough time to move and tidy up. The buyers will want this as short as possible because their loan interest clock starts ticking on recording and funding.

Make sure everyone understands this deadline and it's realistic. You don't want a buyer trying to move in the same time you're moving out. This can happen when both buyers and sellers try to move in the same weekend.

Use the deadline checklist in Figure 4-1 to keep track of their due dates.

FIGURE 4-1 Purchase contract deadlines checklist.	
Item	**Deadline Date**
Purchase Contract Acceptance, Counter, or Reject Deadline	
Counter Deadline (1)	
Counter Deadline (2)	
Buyer's Loan Applications and Fees Deadline (hopefully this is done)	
Seller Disclosures Due Date	
Evaluations and Inspections	
Loan Denial Deadline	
Appraisal Deadline	
Closing or Settlement Date	
Time and Date You Have to Be Out and Give the Buyers the Keys	

Next, like the commercials on your favorite TV show, offers you don't like are sure to happen. Here's how to deal with them.

Putting Together Counter Offers

The first step in dealing with an offer you don't like is to make a list of the items you find unacceptable. Then decide on the changes you'll need to make

For instance, suppose the price you're asking is $310,900, but the offer is $295,000. After sharpening the pencil and working the numbers, you come up with $300,000 as the minimum price you can live with.

Next item on the offer is a 60-day closing, but you think this is too long. You don't want an extended closing at your expense. Because the buyers are preapproved they should be able to close in three to four weeks, so you counter with a 30-day closing.

The buyers also want the refrigerator and your John Deere power weed-eater. The refrigerator they can have, but not your John Deere, so that too goes into the counter offer. What you've written on the counter form should look something like this:

1. Purchase price to be $300,000.

2. Closing date to be on or before March 30, 2005.

3. Refrigerator is included as part of the sale.

4. John Deere power weed-eater is not included in the sale.

5. All other terms and conditions remain the same.

6. Buyers have until 5:00 P.M. of the following day to respond.

You sign the form and it goes back to the buyers. If they sign it, it's a done deal. It could also come back as a counter-counter offer and then it starts all over again.

Getting Emotional Can Cost You a Deal

It's important to realize that some people start out the buying process by writing a low offer, hoping you'll counter up to your lowest price. It's just the way they operate—nothing personal or vindictive—just something a friend or relative put into their heads that this is the way you buy a home. They're scared they'll lose the home, but this is the way Uncle Joe said you do it, so they write a low offer with sweaty palms.

If your counter is reasonable for the market, and if the buyers are serious, they'll usually take it.

An offer can also be low because that's all the buyers are qualified for. They may also have a second or third choice in mind or may be trying to get the best deal possible. Sometimes it's hard to tell what their motivation is.

In one particular example, a buyer came in with an offer that was $10,000 low on a home that was priced at fair market value. The sellers were so upset that they raved for fifteen minutes about all they had done to the house and how ignorant these buyers were because they couldn't appreciate it. Finally, they cooled down enough to tell their agent they wanted to reject the offer and not counter. She talked them into countering and adding back in $9,800, but throwing in the washer, dryer, lawnmower, hoses, and garden tools. They had bought a condo and were planning on leaving or giving the tools and equipment away anyway.

Although everyone expected the buyers to walk away, they accepted the counter. As it turned out, they were happy to get the appliances and everything they needed to maintain the yard. But most importantly, they felt they had won in the negotiating. They happily told their friends about all the equipment they had gotten the owner to throw in to make the deal.

The key is not to get into an ego battle with a buyer, but to focus on the goal of selling the house.

In another situation, sellers angrily rejected a low-ball offer with unreasonable deadlines. They checked the rejection box with a big red X and sent it back to the buyers hoping to never hear from them again.

To everyone's amazement, the buyer's agent called and demanded to know why their offer was rejected and why it wasn't countered like they expected. The listing agent explained that they would need to make a much better offer if they wanted it taken seriously and to try again.

The next day a new and better offer came in. It still wasn't acceptable to the sellers but they did counter back this time and it was accepted.

The point is to corral the emotions so they don't get in the way. True, it's normal to get downright angry when people get excited over your decorating and how nice your home is then come in thousands of dollars under your asking price.

It's a personal rejection, like being turned down for the junior prom or passed over for a job promotion. You'll feel the buyers are idiots, why can't they see all the work you've put into the house, the decorating and colors you spent so much time deciding on, and the memories you've created in this home. These feelings are natural, and all sellers go through them when they get a low offer.

Vent your anger and walk around the block, but calm down before responding. It's important to focus on your goal of selling the house. Obviously, the buyers liked something about your home or they wouldn't go to the trouble of writing an offer.

Another important part of the counter-offer process is contingencies. How to handle them is important to your closing check.

Dealing with Contingencies

Contingencies are clauses written into an offer that make it subject to something happening, such as the buyers qualifying for financing, selling their home, or you paying some of their closing costs. They can be standard clauses in the purchase contract that are activated by checking a box, by writing on a blank line, or adding a separate addendum. (See Figure 4-2 for a list of the most common contingencies.)

FIGURE 4-2
Common contingencies to real estate offers.

Contingency	Details
Third-Party Approval of Property	Buyers want someone to check out the property and give their stamp of approval. Uncle Joe, the builder, for example.
Third-Party Approval of Sales Contract	Usually an attorney or financial advisor. Sometimes it's parents putting up the cash for first-time buyers.
Subject to Home Appraising for Sales Price	If the appraisal comes in low, the buyer can walk away, or you can meet the appraised price by writing up an addendum.
As-Is Condition	Buyer offers to purchase the property as-is with no repairs.
Home Inspection	If repairs are needed, you'll get an addendum from the buyers listing what's needed to make them happy. You can accept or counter what's on the list.
Subject to Seller Buying Another Home	Sellers put this in to protect them from becoming homeless if their offer on another home falls through or if they need to find another home before closing. There's usually a time limit for all this to happen.
Subject to Buyer's Home Selling or Closing	The offer on your home is subject to the buyers' selling or closing on their home. You'll want a time limit on this.
Time Clause	If you accept an offer subject to a buyer's home selling, you add in a clause that gives the buyer two to three days to perform if you get a better offer.
Credit Report, Loan Approval, etc.	These have time limits, and it's best to remove them with an addendum as they are completed.
Buying a New Home	All changes, additions, and deadline extensions between you and the builder should be in writing.

As each contingency is fulfilled, it should be "removed in writing" with an addendum. This is especially important on those items that have a time limit or where the earnest-money check is forfeited if the deal falls through.

For example, if the offer is subject to a buyer's loan approval, you'll want to remove that contingency with an addendum as soon as the lenders tell you it is approved. You simply write on the form that the offer is no longer subject to loan approval and both parties date and sign. This protects you in case the deal falls through at the last minute because the buyer can't perform. You are entitled to the deposit because you took your home off the market and lost weeks of valuable selling time.

If you've listed your home with a Realtor, she will handle this paperwork so all you have to do is sign off as the items are completed.

However, if you're selling FSBO, you'll want to have at least five or more multipart addendum forms on hand for possible counters and contingency removals. Even with full-price offers you'll have a few "subject-to" clauses to deal with. But, be aware that you can make just about anything a subject-to by attaching an addendum to the offer.

The Full-Price Offer

Full-price offers can also be perilous at times. When a full-price offer comes quickly, sellers often wonder if they priced the home too low.

If you've done your homework and priced it at market, it could be that you've gotten lucky. If your home is exactly what a buyer is looking for, a full-price offer is not unusual.

In one instance, a seller got a full-price offer about 45 minutes after the home went on the multiple listing. Instead of being happy the seller was upset. He felt the home must be underpriced, the agents were getting a windfall without doing anything, and he mentally wasn't prepared. He had assumed it would take a few weeks after putting the home on the market before anything would happen.

The buyer's agent had to explain that he was working with a family who wanted to be close to parents living on the seller's street. They happened to be checking the multiple listing when the property came up and they acted quickly. It took a couple of days of assurances, but the seller finally accepted the offer and the deal closed.

Once you decide to put your home on the market, anything can happen. There's a constant flow of buyers and houses circulating on the market. Someone could have their eye on your neighborhood waiting for a home to go up for sale because it's close to family or work.

One pitfall to look out for is full-price offers from unqualified buyers. Sellers sometimes get so excited that they don't look at the total picture. Buyers who are not prequalified or who have a house to sell first can cause serious problems if they tie your house up and the deal falls through. Months of prime selling time can go down the drain as well as create havoc with your plans.

In one particular situation, homeowners selling FSBO took their home off the market for six months while working with a buyer who was trying to get qualified. When asked why they let the buyer string them along for so long, the homeowners replied, "Because the buyer came in with a full-price offer."

What if the Buyer Has a Home to Sell First?

Another contingency that can cause a lot of problems is when buyers must sell their home before they can buy yours. With this contingency, a buyer makes an offer, usually full price or more, but will specify that the offer is subject to their home selling. Is this a bad thing? Not always. What you want to avoid is tying up your home for a period of time and then have the deal fall apart because your home's buyers can't sell theirs.

If your home is in a price range that's slow selling, but the buyer's home is in a lower price bracket that sells faster, it can be an advantage. On the other hand, if the buyer's home is in a similar bracket to yours, all you'll do is jump from one frying pan to another equally as hot.

Before you make that jump, here are some suggestions:

■ If you're in a hot market, you probably won't gain a lot by waiting for a buyer's home to sell. If you do want to put a deal together, put in a clause that you can keep the home on the market. If another buyer comes along with a great offer, the first buyer has x amount of time—usually 48 to 72 hours—to perform; if they don't, their offer terminates. In real estate speak this is called a time clause.

■ It's a slow market and your buyer's home is in a faster-selling price bracket. This can be a good thing. In essence, you've jumped into a slightly cooler frying pan. Still, you'll want to keep your home on the market with a time clause if possible.

■ Make sure you've got a good earnest money deposit. If you have to wait for a buyer to sell their home, you don't want them to string you along for months and then have a change of heart.

■ Do the same pricing homework on the buyer's home that you did when you put your home on the market. You don't want to tie your home up if the buyer's home is overpriced or not in good, sale-able condition.

■ Make sure the buyers can qualify for your home if their home sells. Do the math so you know what their equity is, and require them to prequalify for the loan to buy your home.

■ Too many sellers go for long shots when they get a full-price or better offer, and in their enthusiasm fail to look at the what-ifs. Your monthly payment meter still racks up those daily interest charges, and a meltdown of your sale can be expensive.

Next, what's better than a full-price offer? How about several offers competing for your signature on the acceptance line.

How to Handle Multiple Offers

Too much of a good thing, like several offers on your home at once, can bring on a panic attack. Actually, if you've got your home in top selling condition and it's a hot market, it's almost certain you'll end up with several offers the first day it's on the market. In really hot markets, the decision can boil down to how much over asking price the offer is—10 percent to 20 percent or more over asking price is not uncommon.

Should you be so lucky, here's how you can handle this situation:

1. Have your Realtor inform all parties that there are x number of offers on the property. If you're selling the home on your own, then you'll be informing all interested parties that you'll be looking at all offers on a certain day and time.

2. If you're working with an agent, his or her office would be a neutral place to meet with the buyer's agents and go over the offers. When you're selling your home yourself, have the buyers to drop off their offers by the deadline.

3. Go over the offers and pick out the one that best meets your needs as to price, terms, deadlines, and closing date. If you can live with it, great. Sign it. If it's not quite right, counter it with a time limit for the buyers to accept it or reject it.

Next, take the second best offer and also counter it. Make sure you write in the counter offer that it's a back-up offer #2 and will kick in if offer #1 rejects your counter. It should also have a time limit for acceptance. Offer #3 and any other offers are handled the same way.

4. If the first counter offer accepts, you've got the home sold on your terms. If the buyer of the first counter says no, then the one making the second counter offer gets an opportunity to accept or reject, and so on down the line. With this approach, all parties are treated fairly and you end up with the best offer possible with the least amount of brain damage.

Nate and Eleni—selling their home FSBO—dealt with multiple offers when they sold their $375,000 four-bedroom, three-bath ranch in a superheated market. They decided to kick off their marketing with an ad in an area weekly that comes out on Friday mornings. Five couples came by Friday afternoon and three on Saturday morning. By noon they had four offers in hand and one more on the way.

This is how these sellers handled the offers:

First, Nate told each party that came through they would cut off accepting offers at 3:00 P.M., Saturday.

Second, at 3:00 P.M. Nate and Eleni sat down and went over the five offers. The first three offers they eliminated. One was less than the asking price, another was subject to a home selling in another state, and on the third there was no information about the buyers having prequalified for a loan.

The remaining two were good offers and both had financing verifications attached. One was for $385,500 with a 60-day escrow, and the other was $385,000 and a 30-day escrow.

Nate and Eleni chose to go with the buyer offering a 30-day escrow because their loan payment was $1,798 a month and of that $1,540 was interest. Even with the slightly higher price, it would cost them another month's interest or $1,040 to go with a 60-day escrow.

So what's a quick way to determine which offer's the best one? It's easy: Tally up the numbers on the seller's worksheet shown in Figure 4-3.

Using a Net Sheet to Compare Offers

When you compare offers, it can be tricky and you won't know which offer is the best unless you do the math.

To make sure your numbers are accurate, call a title company you've hopefully lined up and find out what the closing costs will be for your sales price. Also, get loan payoffs from your mortgage company. With this data on hand, you can figure accurately what you'll walk away with.

Even if your home is listed with a Realtor, you'll still want to work up your own net sheet to avoid any surprises at closing.

FIGURE 4-3
Seller's worksheet.

SELLER'S WORKSHEET

☺ Sales Price   (1) $ _____

Less Selling Costs

☹ 1ˢᵗ Mortgage Balance $ _____ (Pmt $_____)

☹ 2ⁿᵈ Mortgage Balance $ _____ (Pmt $_____)

☹ Commissions $ _____

☹ Title Insurance $ _____

☹ Transfer Fees or Tax $ _____

☹ Escrow/ Closing Fees $ _____

☹ Mortgage Interest $ _____

☹ Property Tax Proration $ _____

☹ Recording $ _____

☹ Buyer Concessions $ _____

☹ Other _____ $ _____

☹ Total Selling Costs: (2) $ _____

☺ Estimated Proceeds from Sale (the bottom line):   (3) $_____

To figure what you'll net from an offer, fill in the offer price on line (1) then add up all the costs associated with the sale and total (2). Subtract (2) from (1) to get (3) about what your closing check will be.

If getting multiple offers seems stressful, just remember it could be worse trying to sell in a slow market. The next section discusses how to handle slow markets and entice buyers with concessions.

Attracting Offers in a Slow Market

A slow market is created by more homes chasing fewer buyers. This kind of market happens when a major employer leaves, when the area is overbuilt, when interest rates are high, when the local or national economy is in a slump, or even sometimes can be caused by bad weather.

Suppose the market in your area tanks. The number of people buying homes drops by 20 percent, to take an extreme example. But, that leaves 80 percent of potential home buyers still making offers. The key becomes positioning your home to be enticing to that 80 percent still buying homes.

True, buyers have many more homes to choose from, but those that suffer most will be in marginal condition, in less desirable areas, or overpriced.

Since there are more homes in the inventory, you'll need to be a little more competitive and be willing to make more concessions. However, a word of caution: The best way to use concessions is when you're negotiating an offer. If you advertise or offer them up front, you may end up with buyers who make low offers and want the concessions too.

So what do you do to entice buyers to choose your home over the one down the street? You sweeten the pot.

How to Sweeten the Pot

Here are some things you can do to add a touch of honey so buyers will make an offer or take your counter:

- The number one sweetener is the home's condition: fresh paint, like-new floors, great curb appeal, and so on. Start working on these items a month or two before you put your home on the market.

- Price your home right at market value. Adding so-called wiggle room to the price can make you uncompetitive and lose potential buyers.

- Offer to pay the buyer's closing costs, between $2\frac{1}{2}$ to 3 percent of the loan amount.

- Throw in appliances or other items the buyers may want. If your appliances are several years old, it may be a plus to replace them with more energy-efficient models rather than to move them. Plus you save the cost of moving them.

  In one particular sale the seller threw in a big screen TV and pool table to make the deal work. Fortunately, the buyers went for it because the seller had finished the basement family room after he hauled in the TV and pool table. There was no way to get them out short of disassembly or serious demolition. In another deal the Realtor took a boat for his commission where the seller wanted to take a lower offer, which wouldn't leave him with enough equity to cover the fee.

■ If a buyer doesn't like your carpet color or decor, offer to replace it up to a certain dollar amount. Typically, this can run from $2,500 on up depending on price range and area.

   This is different from an allowance that some sellers use to avoid fixing problems like bad carpets or old paint. When you do this, you'll likely end up with a bargain hunter wanting the allowance and making a low offer too.

■ Offer an extended closing date of 60 to 90 days. This can be enticing for buyers moving from another area where they have to close on their home first. It can also work if the buyers have a few months left on an apartment lease.

■ If a buyer has a month or two left on their lease, you can offer to help buy out the lease so they can buy your home.

■ Better than extending the closing date is to close and rent back from the new owners for whatever time would be a win-win for both of you. The monthly rent would be the buyer's mortgage payment. This could be a plus by giving you additional time to find another home or build one. Plus, you've sold the home, closed, the money is in the bank, and your stress level is way down.

If you're selling FSBO, listen to the buyers who come through. Let them talk and note what their needs are so you can effectively respond to any offers or counters. Likewise, if you're working with an agent, have her talk to the buyer's agent and get as much information as possible. This may not be critical in a sellers market, but in a slow market you may have only one chance to make a sale and you don't want to lose it.

Keep in mind that listing with a Realtor can be the best way to go in a slow market because they have access to qualified buyers and because cooperating agents can hammer out deals that may otherwise never happen. It can boil down to whether you're better off paying money in commissions or slashing your selling price to attract bargain hunters.

Time Is Not in Your Favor

When you get an offer you should treat it like opening a can of Pepsi: You've got about an hour before the fizz is gone. Buyers in a slow market usually have more than one home on their short list. So, if you get an offer, know your bottom line, mortgage payoffs, and closing costs so you can act swiftly with an acceptance or counter offer. Don't assume because buyers have made an offer that they've stopped looking.

It may be written on the paperwork that you have 48 hours to decide, but remember they can withdraw their offer anytime before you've signed it. Too many sellers see they've got x amount of time on the offer and relax. And many buyers don't shift out of search mode until their offer is signed and delivered. There are a lot of real estate war stories where buyers have made an offer and then stumbled upon another house they liked better. Their agent has to frantically call the selling agent and tell him the buyers are withdrawing their offer.

Experienced buyer agents will often write "upon presentation" in the line for how long the seller has to respond. They do that so the sellers can't use the offer to push a fence-sitting buyer they may have into making a better offer. In real estate speak this is called shopping the offer.

In short, even though the offer may give you x hours to respond, think of opening the can of Pepsi and accepting or countering immediately to stop the buyer from further shopping.

Similar to selling in a slow market is working with buyers with no down payment. It can be frustrating, but it can be rewarding too when it all comes together.

Working with Buyers with Little or Nothing Down

In some hot markets, sellers aren't concerned with marginal buyers with little or no down payment. There are so many buyers chasing the few properties for sale that it's the law of the jungle—you have the bucks lined up and can afford to go several percent over asking price or you stay a tenant.

For the rest of the country, dealing with buyers who have little or no down payment may be the difference between selling and not selling your home.

Two situations you'll likely run into are those who need help with closing costs and those with good credit and job but lacking a down payment.

Paying Buyer's Closing Costs

Many sellers get upset when an offer comes in requiring them to pay the buyer's closing costs. They don't understand why they should pay $2\frac{1}{2}$ to 3 percent of the sale price to help someone buy their home.

Well, here are three reasons why paying closing costs can make a sale:

1. In a slow market, there are fewer buyers making offers. To be competitive you may have to entice a buyer to choose your home over the one down the street.

2. If the market for your home is primarily first-time home buyers, you cast a wider net and appeal to more prospects.

3. Lower interest rates are enticing more buyers into the market, but for many the biggest obstacle is the down payment. If you're willing to be creative you can often make a deal work. Some of the costs are offset when you figure in how much interest you save by not waiting for the perfect buyer.

You may also be able to increase the price to cover some of the buyer's concession. For example, suppose a buyer makes an offer on your $175,000 home with a contingency that you pay $5,250 to cover their closing costs so they can buy your home. Essentially, this reduces the money you get at closing by $5,250. You don't want to take that big a bite out of your equity, but you're willing to split it in half and pay $2,625.

But, the buyer can't come with the extra funds needed, so you increase the price $2,620 from $175,000 to $177,625. In reality, the buyer is financing half of the closing costs by taking out a bigger loan.

If your home is listed, your agent and the selling Realtor will negotiate back and forth, each knowing the needs and capabilities of their clients to put a workable deal together. On the other hand, if you're selling FSBO you'll need to work with your prospects and their mortgage lender to hammer out numbers they can qualify for. See Figure 4-4 for buyer concessions that can help you make a deal.

Also critical to the process is the buyer's credit score (credit scoring is covered in Chapter 6, Financing and Money Matters for Sellers). If it's lower than 620 there's no use going any further. To continue on with this buyer will be like working out on a treadmill with the power off.

Next, if you have to cover not only the closing costs but the down payments as well, you need to plan on making concessions of 6 percent

FIGURE 4-4
Buyer concessions that can help you make a deal.

Concession	What It Costs You
Closing Costs	These costs typically run from 1½ percent to 2 percent of the loan amount. In starter homes, where buyers need to go with zero-down programs, costs can go 6 percent or more. You may want to up the price to cover some of them.
Painting and Carpeting	It's better to do this upfront in neutral colors. But, in the event your decor doesn't fit the buyer's furniture or taste, offer the concession as closing credit or as a check at closing.
Extended Closing Dates	Offering 60 to 90 days to close can be a deal maker for someone moving in from another area or someone who has a lease agreement with a few months left to go.
Renting Back After Closing	If both buyer and seller need more time, this is the best way to go. You'll have the home sold and closed as well as time to move. Rent payment is usually the buyer's monthly mortgage payment.
Throwing in Appliances	For first-time home buyers this can be especially effective. They don't have to go shopping, and if your appliances are getting old, using them to make a deal becomes a good way to go.
Offering a Home Warranty or Picking Up the Cost of Professional Home Inspection	This is especially effective if your home is ten or more years old. Let the buyer pick the inspector of their choice. Costs will run around $250 to $450 each.
Selling the Sizzle, not the Steak	Some sizzle items you can sweeten the deal with are cars, boats, cruises, etc. If you're in the travel business you can add a free cruise to attract buyers. Whatever you think will appeal to buyers will work. What's cheap to you may not be to other people.
Selling a Home Contingency	The seller makes an offer subject to their home selling. In short, you take your home off the market for a specified period of time. If the buyer's home doesn't sell, you're back to square one.

to 7 percent of the sales price. For instance, if your sales price is $150,000, the buyer's costs would be around $9,000. As mentioned above, some of this you may have to absorb, and some you can cover by raising the price. How much depends on the appraisal and what the buyers qualify for.

Third-Party Down-Payment Programs

Two typical no-down programs are the Nehemiah and Neighborhood Gold plans mentioned in Chapter 2. They work with FHA, conventional, and sub-prime lenders to gift the down payment and closing costs. Two Web sites for more information on these programs are: *www.thebuyersfund.com* and *www.getdownpayment.com*.

As an example, Anthony and Sandra wanted to buy a home but had no money for down payment or closing costs. A mortgage lender told them about the no-down programs and suggested they make an application. Because of their good credit they were approved for $165,000.

A slow market had created a good selection of homes in their price range and they looked at about twenty homes before zeroing in on a cute, well-decorated bi-level. To get the ball rolling, their Realtor presented a full-price offer but attached an addendum asking the sellers to pay a $9,240 concession so the buyers could go with the Nehemiah program.

The sellers weren't too happy with the offer, but with stiff competition in their price range plus a job transfer looming they knew they would have to make some tough concessions if they wanted to get out of town anytime soon.

The seller's agent felt that increasing the price $3,700 would be about as high as they could go and still have the home appraise. (See Chapter 2 for more about this problem.) This would effectively reduce the seller's concessions to $5,540, an amount they could live with.

When such offers come in, it's important to dampen the knee-jerk reaction to reject them, feeling the buyers are trying to scam you and get into a home with little down. In most cases the buyers are first-time home buyers and don't have the funds needed for down payment and closing costs. But, if you work with these buyers and follow up with their mortgage lender or agent you can often put a deal together.

For example, in one sale an offer came in asking for $7,500 in seller concessions. The seller's agent talked to the mortgage lender and their appraiser and was able to reduce the concessions to $2,900. The lender did this by increasing the price and reducing their fees where possible to make the deal work.

Even better is when you can tap into funds some local governments are willing to give first-time home buyers to live in their cities.

Using Local Grant Programs as a Selling Tool

Many cities and counties have community grant/loan programs that help first-time home buyers buy a home. Some of these programs are for targeted areas, others are city-wide programs. These loans are typically FHA guaranteed and follow their underwriting standards.

To find out what grant programs are available in your area, go to *www.HUD.gov.* Find the Local Information tab, scroll down, and click on your state. Under the red tab, you'll find a list of communities with home-buying programs in your state.

If you live in a grant area and are selling FSBO, it'll pay to check out what's available. These programs can increase the buyer pool you have to work with. For example, Goran and Nada went the community-grant route when they wanted to buy a home but didn't have much of a down payment. The city they lived in had a program that would pay up to $4,000 to help first-time home buyers in targeted areas. If the buyers lived in the home for five years the loan was forgiven.

The local real estate market was slow and had a good supply of homes for sale to choose from. Goran and Nada found a home they liked and made an offer that called for the seller to pay $2,600 of their closing costs. It was an offer the sellers eagerly accepted because their new home was just about completed and the pressure to sell was approaching critical mass. With a $2,600 seller concession added to the $4,000 community grant, the buyers had $6,400 and needed only $720 of their own money to close.

It's hard to keep track of what these concessions cost you and what you're including and not including in the offer. The best way is to do what aircraft pilots do before takeoff: Use a checklist. The one shown in Figure 4-5 will keep you from crashing.

Purchase Contract Checklist

Purchase agreements, earnest-money agreements, real estate sales contracts, or whatever they're called in your state, have much in common.

FIGURE 4-5
Sales contract checklist.

Item	Action You Need to Take
Earnest Money	No real estate contract is complete without consideration. Make sure the check is attached to the paperwork.
Items You Agree to Leave	This includes items that are not attached to property, such as refrigerator, washer, etc. List each item along with model # so you can give the buyers a bill of sale at closing.
Items You Are Not Including in the Sale	List all items not included, such as that antique chandelier. Make sure it's in writing and specific. Attach digital photos so there's no doubt.
"Subject-to" Clauses	Make sure you understand what the offer is subject to, such as appraisal, financing, inspections, or third-party approvals.
Closing and Possession Dates	Note the closing and possession dates and whether they will work for you. Monday, Tuesday, or Wednesday are the best days to close.
Seller Disclosures	If your state requires you to fill out property disclosure forms, note how much time you have to get them to the buyer.
Buyer's Deadlines	In some states, the buyer has deadlines for loan approvals, appraisals, etc., or they can lose their deposit if the deal fails. Note these dates and keep them as tight as possible.
Look for Clauses That Refer to Addendums	Make sure all addendums are accounted for and numbered 1/X, 2/X, etc.
Who Pays for What?	Note the clauses that specifies who pays for appraisal, inspections, home warranties, and so on.
Counter Offer	Check box or indicate that you've written a counter on addendum 1/X. Also, write in a deadline for accepting the counter.
Additional Addendums	Make sure you have all the disclosure addendums required, such as federal lead-based paint, FHA financing, and other state and local required forms. All addendums need to be signed by both parties and numbered 1/X.
Letter from Buyer's Lender	You should verify buyer's financing before you accept or counter any offer.
Work Up the Numbers Before You Sign	Fill out the Sellers Net Worksheet (Figure 4-3) to find your bottom line.

The wording may differ and there may be a few items unique to your state, but the basics are the same. The checklist in Figure 4-6 will keep you on track when you get an offer so you won't miss anything critical.

Home Warranties and Inspections Can Be a Great Sales Tool

Home warranties can be both a sales tool and a liability-limiting tool. If you have an older home, buyers may question the condition of the home's plumbing, heating, electrical, and other components. You can try to convince them it's in good condition or you can offer a home warranty good for one year.

Interestingly, a recent National Home Warranty Association survey of the California market found 56 percent of the sellers' buying

FIGURE 4-6
The art of the deal summary checklist.

Item	Action Needed
You Get an Offer	Make sure it is in writing, signed by all parties, with an earnest-money check attached.
Is the Buyer Qualified?	Preapproval letter from lender attached. Doesn't hurt to call lender and verify information on letter.
Are the Deadlines, Especially for Closing and Possession, Acceptable?	Check the purchase contract carefully to make sure you don't miss any fine print.
What Happens if You Counter?	You don't want to give the buyer more than 8 to 12 hours to accept, counter, or reject your counter offer.
You're Mad As Hell Because of a Low Offer	Don't x the reject box. Take some time and cool down. Many deals are put together with a counter and a cool head.
You Get an Offer with You Paying Some Buyer's Costs	Do the math and see if you can work it out by raising the price. Have a can-do attitude. It may take a couple of counters to reach a deal.

policies did so to avoid potential lawsuits, complaints, and disclosure problems arising from the sale.

Likewise, a professional home inspection can help limit your liability. Usually the buyer pays for a home inspection, but there's no reason you can't offer an inspection as a sales tool to tip the scales in your favor.

How Home Warranties Work

For a one-time fee of from $250 to $500, you get a one-year insurance policy covering electrical, heating, and plumbing systems. Also included are built-in appliances such as dishwashers, disposals, compactors, and range/ovens. Refrigerators, air conditioners, washers, and dryers usually are not included in the basic coverage of most policies, but can be covered at additional cost. Since plans can vary, check to make sure all items important in your home are included or can be covered with a rider.

With most programs, if you have a problem you call the warranty company, which sends a repair person from its own local network of contractors. Usually they'll charge a service fee of $35 to $50.

The major benefit of a warranty is protection from problems you don't know exist, such as a cracked furnace heat chamber, water heater, or air conditioner going out within a year of closing. Even though you've filled out disclosures and the buyer has hired a home inspector, a warranty is another layer of protection from the buyer coming back and saying you didn't tell them the water heater or whatever was defective. The year-coverage of a home warranty should prevent this from happening.

It's important to realize that most warranties don't cover structural repairs, such as a roof or foundation. There are, however, a growing number of companies that do offer—for a higher premium—coverage for structural and roofing work. Also, coverage of plumbing systems varies widely. Some policies cover all pipes—inside the home and out—but others don't. You'll need to read the fine print to find out what's covered.

One of the most important policy restrictions to look for is "preexisting conditions." Many warranty programs don't cover problems that may have been present and detectable before the policy went into effect. The coverage varies widely, so it's important to read and compare policies carefully before buying.

Regulation of home warranties varies from state to state. In some states, the real estate commission is the regulator, but in others the department of insurance has jurisdiction. Also, the many different companies and policies have created confusion about what is and isn't covered. As a result, many consumers have the misconception that a home warranty covers everything down to a leaky faucet. In reality, the only way to find out what you're getting is to read the policy over carefully and verify the company's financial stability.

Different regions require different emphasis on what is covered. In the Sun Belt, for example, air-conditioning and pool coverage are important, but in the Northeast furnaces and sprinkler systems would be a primary concern. Regardless of the area you live in, the important things to look for in choosing a policy are:

1. Make sure the insurer is financially sound and has a good track record. The best policy is worthless if the company goes bankrupt. Look for companies tied in with substantial national corporations that usually advertise in your local yellow pages. It's a plus if the warranty company is a member of the National Home Warranty Association (NHWA).

Check with a real estate broker or two for companies they have had good experiences with. Also, it doesn't hurt to verify customer references or check financial filings at the department of real estate or insurance.

2. Read the policy through and make sure you understand what is and is not covered as well as what the company charges for the service fee. On the average, most service fees run in the $35 to $50 range. But remember, it's a matter of trade-offs, and the lowest service fee is not always the best deal.

3. Look carefully at the "preexisting conditions" part of the policy. Does the insurer require a presale home inspection before the policy becomes effective, and is there a time period before certain items are covered after the buyer moves in?

4. Make sure the optional coverage you want—such as swimming pool, air conditioning, or refrigerator—is included.

Even though warranties can be a good sales tool and give you some protection, home inspections give you an even better protection layer. And there's no reason you can't use this as a buyer inducement as well. The next section tells how.

Offers Are Often Subject to Home Inspections

Even though most states require sellers to disclose problems in writing to a buyer, it boils down to the seller's opinion about the condition of the house and its components. There may be problems you're not aware, which can come back and cause you headaches down the road. To minimize this, a professional home inspection can add another layer of protection and double as a sales tool. It'll cost you $250 to $475, but it goes a long way toward reducing the risk of selling an existing home.

Sometimes sellers of older homes are apprehensive about inspections, having heard they must bring a home up to code before they can sell. Not so. Generally, sellers are not required to be code compliant when they sell unless it's required in an offer.

But if you're selling an older home, having both written disclosure and a home inspection can be good insurance if problems develop and the buyer wants to blame you.

Also, is it better to hire an inspector up front or give the buyer a credit to hire one of their choosing? Sellers have successfully gone both ways.

If you do get an inspection up front, go with a reputable company that buyers will feel comfortable with, preferably a member of ASHI or NIBI. You don't want to give any impression that the inspection is not objective.

Also, having an inspection up front lets you know whether there are any problems you'll need to take care of before you get an offer.

Finding a Home Inspector
To find a home inspector, check the yellow pages in your area or the following Web sites: *www.ashi.com* (American Society of Home Inspectors) and *www.nibi.com* (National Institute of Building Inspectors),

On the other hand, letting the buyer choose the inspection company certainly removes you from any liability for the inspection and puts it on the buyer's shoulders.

Those are the trade-offs and you'll have to decide what fits your situation best.

Regardless of who chooses the inspector, most buyers are making their offers subject to a professional inspection. And the reality is that a bad report can give the buyer reason to cancel the sale and get their deposit back. Though far more frequently, they'll use the report to get you to renegotiate the offer and/or correct any problems.

Typically, home inspectors, in their search for problems, will spend a couple of hours going over the home and then write up a report detailing any mechanical, structural, or safety problems they've found. Some inspectors want the buyers to be there, others don't. Either way, plan on finding something to do for two or three hours while the inspector crawls around your house.

Home buyers Alan and Sandra had an interesting experience when they wrote an offer on a twelve-year-old home in an upscale neighborhood. It was exactly what they were looking for. They felt so lucky to find the home that they didn't want to jeopardize their offer by making it subject to an inspection. However, their agent insisted on the contingency, stressing that a few hundred dollars is cheap insurance when you're investing over $350,000.

A few days later the inspector met the buyer's agent at the home, and what should have been a routine inspection turned up major problems. The house had been damaged in a fire about eight years before and the repairs were less than professional. Several joists in the attic were charred and should have been replaced. Likewise, damaged wall studs had been sheet rocked over in an obvious attempt to repair cheaply.

When the sellers were offered a chance to have a contractor redo the repairs and save the sale, they refused. This was a big disappointment for the buyers, but they were glad they were saved a costly mistake.

For the sellers it was an unappreciated blessing, because they most certainly would have ended up with a lawsuit if the sale had closed.

In another example, Scott and Marissa's inspection report came back with several small but serious problems, such as an improperly installed furnace flue, no flex connector or strapping securing the water heater, and no vents in the door to the furnace room.

In this case, the seller agreed to pay a heating contractor to correct the problems before closing. Typically, most problems are handled this way because the sellers realize they have to take care of them or the house won't sell.

Once problems have been disclosed and documented, you can't claim ignorance on future disclosure forms without leaving yourself open to serious liability. The days of selling as-is with nondisclosure are no more.

In summary, when you get an offer, use the handy checklist in Figure 4-6 so you don't overlook anything vital to a successful deal.

Have a can-do attitude. It may take a couple of counters to reach a deal.

CHAPTER 5

Selling a Condo, Co-Op, or Townhouse

According to the National Association of Realtors, condo, co-op, and townhouse sales from 2001 to 2004 have been record breakers. (In this chapter, I'll refer to all three as "condos" for the sake of brevity, unless otherwise noted.) The main reason for such strong sales is low interest rates, which allow more renters to become homeowners and attract more homeowners who want yard-free living. This is great for condo sellers because their investment can yield a healthy return, something that has not always happened in the past.

Still, there are some differences in selling a condo versus a detached home, which need to be taken into account so you can net the most money possible. The most common differences are:

1. The various units in a condo development are similar enough that it can be difficult to create a competitive difference. If price becomes the dominant selling feature, those who have equity they can sacrifice and who need to sell fast will lower their price. In turn, this brings down the value of all the other units for sale.

2. Many associations restrict *For Sale* signs and open houses. Some ban all signs, whether on the lawn or in the windows, so you'll need to get creative in getting the word out that your condo is for sale.

3. The homeowners association or board also plays an important part in a sale. If the development is well managed, the associa-

tion will have reserves and a budget for maintenance and replacement needs. If it doesn't, buyers will go elsewhere. They don't want to be stuck paying high assessments when something needs replacing.

4. Problems among members of the homeowners association can also dampen sales. Bad publicity or disgruntled owners can spread the word that living in that development is not fun.

5. If the development is a co-op, your buyer will likely need to be approved by the board. This restricts to whom you can sell and what financing options are available.

6. The number of units rented out can have a major impact on your sales plans. If rental units exceed 50 percent, you may have trouble getting lenders to finance sales.

But as with detached homes, the first step in putting your home on the market is get it in top selling condition.

Putting Your Unit in Selling Condition

Since you don't own the building or the amenities—like you would in a detached home—there's not much you can do about the exterior; however, you can make your unit as attractive as possible.

One sales advantage you have is that buyers will frequently look at all the competing units for sale before making a decision. That means prospective buyers looking at another unit will probably look at yours too. If yours shows better, you may snag an offer.

The following checklist will help you make your unit competitive and attract buyers who make the rounds. Go through the other units in your complex that are for sale and compare with yours. Use the following checklist to see how you stack up.

How Does Your Unit Stack Up with Others for Sale?

☐ Look at your entryway. Would some small things like pots of flowers or refinishing your entryway door make it more inviting?

☐ Does your unit need painting or new floor coverings?

☐ Are the appliances in good condition or do they need upgrading? [Note: In condos, appliances are owned by the owners but usually stay with the unit when sold.]

☐ How about window treatments? Do they let in the maximum amount of light and add a cheerful note to your unit?

☐ Do your light fixtures add to your decor or are they dusty originals that need replacing?

☐ Are your kitchen and bath counter tops in good condition?

☐ Do the kitchen cupboards need replacement or refinishing?

☐ If you have a better view than the competing units, exploit it by making sure the window coverings are open when showing the unit.

☐ Remove as much furniture as possible so the unit looks bigger. Declutter with the intent of making it easy for a buyer to visualize themselves living there. Remove and pack anything that can be a distraction, such as photos, pictures, trophies, or collections.

This checklist then becomes a to-do list to get your unit in shape. Next step is to nail down the sales price that'll get you the most money in the shortest time.

Price Your Unit to Get the Most Money

One advantage (or disadvantage) over detached homes is that all similar units for sale are competing on a level playing field; the exteriors, layout, and size are generally the same. Which unit a buyer chooses to make an offer on boils down to three things.

1. *Price* is the first and most powerful consideration. If it's a hot market and all the units are going up in value, you'll ride the price tide up like everyone else. But if it's a slow market, it can get vicious. Sellers with some equity who have to sell will cut their price to the bone. That reduces the value of other similar units to the lowest priced one.

2. Your unit's *condition* is the second consideration. How does it compare to others for sale in the complex? As mentioned above, anything you can do to gain a showing edge is to your advantage.

3. *Location* of your unit in the development is the third consideration. For many buyers this is a critical consideration, and many times they'll pay more for this amenity. Some examples are:

- Does your unit overlook a park or woodland?

- Do you have a lake-, river-, or other water view?

- South-facing windows are often a plus. Most buyers like bright, sunny rooms.

- Does your unit face away from busy streets or other noise generators?

- Do you have good access, such as a ground unit versus a third floor location?

- Do you have good neighbors who get along? In one development, several units sold because the owners in that section had a reputation for being sociable and doing fun things together. This attracted their friends who wanted to be part of it.

So How Do You Set the Price?

First, look at what similar units have sold for in the past few months. If you're in a red-hot market, look at data from the last thirty days, or an even shorter period.

The best way to get this data is talk to two or three agents who have sold units in your complex or who have one or more listed. Ask them what they think your home is worth. Their estimates should be close together.

Next, look at the units that are currently for sale. If you've gone through them and filled out the checklist, you'll know exactly how you stack up. If you're at the top of the food chain you'll be able to price your unit on the high end of what's selling.

A word of caution here: Having one of the best units doesn't guarantee you'll get a lot more money. But, depending on the market, it could mean the difference between selling and not selling, or selling faster than units in not as good condition.

Shelly used this approach when she sold her 7-year-old condo. It was in a good area, so units were selling on average in thirty to sixty days. She talked to two agents who over the past year had sold several condos in the complex. They both suggested the high $170s as a likely selling price.

Because Shelly was serving on the homeowner's association board and had met many of the owners, she had seen their units when she was running for election. She felt her condo was one of the better decorated ones with new paint and floor coverings, and in good overall condition.

Shelly also made it a point to go through the units in her complex that were for sale. Based on her homework she decided to price her condo at $179,900.

Five days into her listing, Shelly received an offer for $179,250. A retired couple who recently sold their four-bedroom home offered cash with a two-week closing. They made an offer on this unit because it was in great condition and they didn't want to spend time fixing up or redecorating—they had other priorities involving their motor home.

Unfortunately, it's not always this easy. If there are a lot of units for sale or the market is slow, you may want to consider listing with an agent.

Advantages of Listing Your Condo or Co-Op on the MLS

If you list your unit with a Realtor, the MLS is especially effective with condos, co-ops, and townhouses. Agents showing units will usually take their clients through all the ones listed.

This can be a two-edged sword that cuts for or against you. On the plus side, if your unit is one of the better ones that you've decorated nicely, it will benefit from the advertising and showing of other listings. And it's likely it will sell more quickly.

On the down side, if your unit needs some TLC then you'll probably end up helping sell one of your neighbor's units. This is one of the realities of selling a condo or co-op versus a detached home, you have fewer areas to compete in. As a result, it's critical to make your unit as attractive as possible.

An important advantage of having a Realtor handle the sale is being able to show your condo to prospective buyers while you're at work or away for the weekend. A Realtor can install an electronic key-box that allows other agents to show your unit when you're not there. This ensures that no buyers are going to slip through your fingers because you were away.

These keyboxes are about half the size of a paperback novel and fit on your doorknob like an oversized padlock. Agents who want to show your unit when you're away will enter their access code via a keypad or infrared device. A tray will pop open with the key, and the agent can now get into the unit, replacing the key in the box when finished.

The keybox records the agent's name, time and date of access, and office phone number. Your agent can electronically retrieve this data and use it to follow up for feedback on how the buyers liked your unit.

In a Slow Market, You Need All the Help You Can Get

In a down market you'll probably need a Realtor. Granted, it'll cost you around 6 percent, but paying a commission is better than not selling or taking a loss that could be greater than the commission fee. Here are four reasons why listing with an agent is a good way to go in a down market:

1. A good Realtor will help you price your unit to be competitive. She knows the market and has the latest sales data. This is vital in a slow market where price can be the only thing that separates you from the others in the development.

2. In a slow market, the MLS attracts qualified buyers because of its large condo inventory. You'll benefit because buyers attracted to your development by other units for sale may end up buying yours.

3. With your condo listed, you won't be pestered by bargain hunters, who prey on FSBOs hoping to get a good deal from an unsuspecting seller.

4. Deals are often hard to come by in a slow market, and having an agent with condo experience can make a big difference. They know how to work with buyers who have little or no money down, bad credit, or other problems.,

It's also true that you can cut the selling price further because you're not paying a commission, but will this offset the MLS advantage of a large pool of buyers? Who knows. There are as many opinions as sellers and agents.

How to Pick an Agent

If you decide to use an agent, be sure to pick a professional with a track record in your area, not one because they're a friend or relative. Too many homeowners go with aunt Susan, uncle Harry, cousin Joe, or a neighbor who just got their real estate license. It's certainly not in your best interest to entrust one of the biggest investments in your life to someone not experienced in selling condos or co-ops.

In short, you want an agent who has a proven track record of selling not just houses, but condos in your development. They're easy to find. Look at the signs or MLS printouts of the units sold or listed in your neighborhood.

Some agents even specialize in certain developments and co-ops. They know the co-op board and their preferences as well as the building. These are the agents you want to seek out and list with. They can guide buyers through the approval paperwork if the co-op requires their approval.

If your condo is new or there isn't any particular agent or company selling in our development, the next chapter will cover in more detail how to find and work with an agent.

Going the FSBO Route

By going FSBO you may be able to save a commission—and that's no small amount. For instance, 6 percent of $185,000 is $11,100, and that comes off your equity. And no, you can't raise the price to compensate. A home is worth what it'll sell and appraise for, and that's what your sales price should be. Buyers really don't care what your selling fees are.

If you're in a hot market where homes sell themselves, it can be a good idea to try it on your own for a week or two. It really doesn't make sense to pay 6 percent when buyers are lining up checkbook in hand wanting to buy your unit. If you don't want to deal with the process, you can shop for an agent who will do it for 3 or 4 percent. Or better still, find one who will do the paperwork for a flat fee when you get an offer from your marketing efforts.

Andrew went the FSBO route when he sold his condo in an upscale complex. It was a hot market, and within hours of running an ad in the local weekly he had three almost identical offers. Two of the offers didn't have prequalification letters, but the third one did. He accepted the third offer because he wanted a sure thing and didn't want to take a chance on buyers who were not preapproved. The sales closed three weeks later and he saved over $9,000 in commissions.

Going FSBO can be a good way to go, and there are effective ways you can get the word out that your condo is for sale. Here are some effective tactics.

Fliers Are a Great Selling Tool

Fliers are an excellent way to bring in buyers. But, because the price and your unit's condition are all that sets you apart from the competition, you'll need to be a little more creative. You'll need to emphasize your unit's value by listing all the things you can think of in your flier that will set you apart from the herd. For example:

- If you've recently installed carpet, tile, or other improvements, list the details. For example, one seller listed an imported Egyptian-tile kitchen floor they recently installed, along with the make and pattern of their upgraded carpets.

- If you have two- or three-tone paint and the other units don't, make a big deal out of it.

- Describe any appliances you've upgraded, providing the make and model number if they're better than the original models or those in other units.

- If you have a better view than many other units, describe it in detail. Let your readers know the view is something to get excited about and a reason to buy your unit.

- Your location in the complex is important. Is it close to the pool or tennis court, or is it quiet because it's at the end of the complex?

- If you have great neighbors, rave about them and anything you do together, such as a yearly barbeque, garage sales, and so on.

- List cell phone numbers on the flier along with your e-mail address. Many people nowadays are using e-mail for first contact, and you don't want to miss a showing.

Of course, it's important to get as many fliers circulating as possible. Keep a supply with you and stick one on every bulletin board you can. Also, pass them out around to other units; someone may have a friend who wants to live in the area.

Ads Are an Effective Sales Tool

In addition to fliers, you'll want to run ads in local papers. Weekly editions seem to work best, probably because the shelf life is longer than for dailies. A simple four- or five-line ad in the "condos for sale" section can bring good results. For example:

Wentworth Garden Condos
3357 Washington Blvd.
3 Bdrms, 2 baths, redecorated.
Fabulous lake view, top level.
$295,950 360-555-3443

When you're writing your ad, remember that buyers are scanning for specific locations, developments, and price ranges. Also, if you've redecorated, if you have a desirable view or other amenities, put that in your ad.

It's also a good idea to put in the price and what level you're on. This will prequalify many callers. It wastes your time to get calls from older couples who want ground floor and you're on the top. Likewise, putting in the price saves you getting calls from buyers outside your price range.

Another ad writing tip is to minimize abbreviations. You may end up paying for an extra line, but spelling out most words makes your ad stand out and easier to read.

If you have a cell phone, put the number in the ad. Yes, it's going to be inconvenient, but only for a week or two until you sell your condo because you were easy to reach.

Showing Your Unit

Calls from your ads or flier can happen anytime, so have voice mail or an answering machine that you can turn on when you're out, If you're listing your cell number and calls sometimes have to go into voice mail, check it often and return calls promptly, since you don't want to miss an opportunity to show your home to a serious buyer.

When you show your unit, it's best to have certain times set aside for showing. Security is important and you'll want someone there with you when you have buyers coming through.

In a sizzling market, the call volume can be overwhelming, so you may want to set up an open house or two and tell callers when they're scheduled to come by. (By scheduling buyers at an open house, you could end up with multiple offers; how to handle these is covered in Chapter 3.)

To help your showings go smoothly you should have a "press kit" put together to give buyers as they come through. In addition to your flier, you'll want to include:

1. A copy of the association's financial statement

2. A copy of the bylaws, CC&R, and articles of incorporation

3. Copies of the minutes for the last six to twelve meetings

4. If possible, a copy of the reserve study that outlines the repairs that can be expected in the future and how much of the current assessment is going into that fund

5. A summary of your last six months' utility bills, or copies of the statements

6. If your state requires a seller's property disclosure—forms used to disclose the condition of the home and its components—include a copy in the press kit

If you have access to a scanner, you can scan your press kit to a PDF file and e-mail it to interested buyers. This can save you and potential buyers a lot of time.

Few sellers will be this well prepared, and your kit will give buyers confidence that you took care of the property and are disclosing everything. In a dead heat between your unit and another, the kit could tip the scales in your favor—people prefer to deal with someone who's professional and on the ball.

Getting an Offer

Another advantage of giving out a press kit is that the buyers have all the information they need to make a clean offer. This means you won't have to scramble to get copies of the HOA (Homeowners Association) financial statements, bylaws, and current rules that a buyer would probably make their offer subject to.

When an offer comes in, use the sales contract checklist in Figure 5-1 to keep focused on what's important to making the deal work.

Once you've gone over the offer, fill in the numbers on the seller's worksheet (Figure 5-2) to find out what you'll walk away with. If you have multiple offers, this can tell you which one is the best deal. See Chapter 3 on how to handle multiple offers.

Dealing with Contingencies

Just like pop-up ads in your e-mail or commercial breaks during your favorite TV program, contingencies will happen. These are clauses written into an offer that make it subject to certain conditions such as appraisals, financing, approvals, etc. They are created by checking a box, filling in a blank line, or writing them on a separate form (addendum). See Chapter 3 for common contingencies and how to handle them. Figure 5-3 covers additional contingencies that apply to sellers and HOAs

Unless it's a hot market, don't be too surprised if an offer comes in low. How to handle these is covered in Chapter 3.

FIGURE 5-1
Sales contract checklist.

Item	Action You Need to Take
Earnest Money	No real estate contract is complete without consideration. Make sure the check is attached to the paperwork.
Items You Agree to Leave That Are Not Attached to Property, such as Refrigerator or Washer	List each item along with model # so you can give the buyers a bill of sale at closing.
Items You Are Not Including in the Sale, such as Antique Chandelier, etc.	List each item, making sure the description is specific. Attach digital photos so there's no doubt.
"Subject-to" Clauses	Make sure you understand what the offer is subject to, such as appraisal, financing, inspections, third-party approvals, condo bylaws.
Closing and Possession Dates	Note the closing and possession dates and make sure they will work for you. Monday, Tuesday, or Wednesday are the best days to close.
Seller's Disclosures	If your state requires you to fill out property disclosure forms, note how much time you have to get them to the buyer.
Buyer's Deadlines	In some states, the buyer has deadlines for loan approvals, appraisals, etc. or they can lose their deposit if the deal fails. Note these dates and keep them as tight as possible.
Addendums	Make sure all addendums are accounted for and numbered 1/x, 2/x, etc., with x being the total number.
Who Pays for What	Note the clauses that specify who pays for appraisal, inspections, home warranties, and so on.
Counter Offer	Check box or indicate that you've written a counter on addendum 1/x. Also, write in a deadline for accepting counter.
Additional Addendums	Make sure you have all the disclosure addendums required, such as federal lead-based paint, FHA financing, and other state and local required forms. All addendums need to be signed by both parties.
Letter from Buyer's Lender	You should verify buyer's financing before you accept or counter any offer.
Work Up the Numbers Before You Sign	Fill out the Seller's Worksheet (Figure 5-2) to find your bottom line. Don't forget to add in any unpaid condo assessments.

FIGURE 5-2
Seller's worksheet.

SELLER'S WORKSHEET

☺ Sales Price   (1) $ _____

Less Selling Costs

☹ 1st Mortgage Balance $ _____ (Pmt $_____)

☹ 2nd Mortgage Balance $ _____ (Pmt $_____)

☹ Commissions $ _____

☹ Title Insurance $ _____

☹ Transfer Fees or Tax $ _____

☹ Escrow/ Closing Fees $ _____

☹ Mortgage Interest $ _____

☹ Property Tax Proration $ _____

☹ Recording $ _____

☹ Buyer Concessions $ _____

☹ Unpaid assessments $ _____

☹ Condo/Co-op Fee Proration $ _____

☹ Other _____ $ _____

☹ Total Selling Costs: (2) $ _____

☺ Estimated Proceeds from Sale (the bottom line):   (3) $_____

To figure what you'll net from an offer, fill in the offer price on line (1) then add up all the costs associated with the sale and total (2). Subtract (2) from (1) to get (3) about what your closing check will be.

FIGURE 5-3
**Common condo and co-op contingencies
to real estate offers.**

Contingency	Details
Third-Party Approvals	Buyers want someone to check out the property and give their stamp of approval. For example, Uncle Joe, the builder, or an attorney. They may also want CPA approval of the condo bylaws or financial statements.
Approval of Condo or Co-Op Paperwork	Usually this involves approval of the rules and restrictions, financial statements, association, or neighbors. It's best to have a short time limit of ten days or less, to be removed with an addendum signed by both parties.
Approval of Buyer	If you need the board's approval of a buyer, this will likely be written on an addendum. When approved, remove the subject-to with another addendum and attach approval letter.
Removal of Appraisal Contingency	Use an addendum after the appraisal is completed.
Seller or HOA Repairs	Repairs can be for your unit or those that are the responsibility of the HOA. Either way, when repairs are completed, buyer inspects and signs removal addendum.
Time Clause	A time clause is usually added to a counter when an offer comes in subject to the buyer's home selling. When another offer comes along, the buyers have x days (say, 3 days) to perform or their offer becomes void.
Home Inspection	The offer is made subject to an acceptable home inspection by a professional or someone designated by the buyer.
Credit Report, Loan Approval, Lender Approval of Condo Development, etc.	These are contingencies dealing with the loan process. It's best to have time limits of five to ten days and remove them by addendum.

CHAPTER 6

Financing and Money Matters for Sellers

It's as important for home sellers to know about financing basics as it is for home buyers. Selling your home and buying another is an integrated project. It's so intertwined that many times sellers will close on their current home and without changing pens sign purchase documents on the next one.

But before that can happen, you'll need to prequalify just like the buyers on your home so you don't run into an ambush after you've gotten an offer. Running into financing problems on your next home with less than a month to go before closing on your present home is not a trip to Disneyland.

In addition, knowing a few financing options—especially if you sell FSBO—can help you create powerful buyer incentives just like the pros use and make you more competitive in a slow market.

For example, how often have you driven by a new subdivision and noticed a banner advertising an interest rate lower than the going rate? Have you wondered how the builder can do that? What's exciting is that you too can advertise lower rates when you sell your home and this chapter shows you how.

You'll also learn about all the other costs and money matters between signing the purchase contract and signing the closing paperwork. This includes how to read the closing statements (HUDs) and how to make sure you're not paying any fees you shouldn't.

But first, a look at financing and credit scoring, and how they effect you as a seller and as a buyer on your next home.

Think About Buying While You're Selling

Even before you put your home on the market, you should be thinking about your next home-buying move. The last thing you want to do is sign a purchase agreement on your home and then find out you can't get into the next home as planned. To make sure this doesn't happen to you, consider these steps before putting your home on the market:

■ Line up a mortgage lender if you haven't done so already and start the preapproval process.

■ When you've decided on a selling price for your home, have your lender work up a Good Faith Estimate (GFE) based on:

1. The price of your next home.

2. Projected down payment from the proceeds of your home plus any other funds you plan on adding.

3. Estimated closing costs.

■ Work up two estimates: one based on your projected sales price and one based on sales price minus 10 percent. This is so you don't run into surprises if you have to pay some concessions or Realtor fees that you hadn't planned on.

■ Use the conservative estimate for your planning. It's much better to get a little more money than expected at closing than a lower figure than you counted on.

When you get all your financial ducks lined up in a neat row, you're ready to plant the *For Sale* sign knowing it's unlikely you'll get caught in a pressure cooker situation.

The first step in avoiding a pressure situation is to understand how credit scoring affects the interest rate and how much you can borrow to get into your next home.

Financing and Credit Scores

Mortgage lenders are often depicted as deal killers who try and find ways to deny applications and keep home buyers from buying their dream house. But in reality, the opposite is true. Lenders work hard and often go the extra mile to get those approvals.

They take your credit and income data and assemble it into a profile of you as a long-term borrower. This data is then shopped to various investors by phone, fax, or e-mail.

Since the mortgage industry is highly competitive and investors are not all alike in their rates and terms, a good mortgage broker will sift through the offers and negotiate the best deal possible in your behalf.

When an investor agrees to make you a loan based on the information provided, they e-mail a commitment to the mortgage broker. Sometimes there are conditions attached, such as your current home selling or requests for additional information.

It's All About Your Credit Score

Because most lending today is Internet based, a credit standard is needed to put everyone on the same page. As a result, credit scoring was developed and has became a universal, though it is sometimes controversial and misunderstood, standard.

FICO scoring, the industry standard, is named after Fair, Isaac and Co., the California-based firm that developed the software. It creates a computer-generated numerical grade that predicts a lender's risk in loaning you money. Your FICO score can change from day to day depending on what information is available from various credit sources.

For more information on credit bureaus and FICO credit scoring, check out:

www.myfico.com

www.creditexpert.com

www.Experian.com

www.Equifax.com

www.Transunion.com

www.icreditreport.com

www.mycreditfile.com

When a mortgage lender orders a credit report, the credit bureaus evaluate and assign a numerical score to five different parts of your credit history.

Two of the five factors relate to your payment history and how much current debt you have, and they make up roughly 65 percent of the score. The length of your credit history, recent credit inquires, and the type of credit you use make up the remaining 35 percent.

FICO scores range from 300 to about 800, and the better your track record is for paying loans back promptly, the higher your score. Typically scores of 720 plus get the best rates and terms. Home buyers with scores in the 620 to 719 range still won't have a problem finding a mortgage, but the interest rates may start to creep up. Scores under 580 are sub-prime territory and interest rates can ratchet up 2 percent or more. Required down payments also climb, sometimes to as high as 30 percent.

When Leon and Tamee applied for a $230,000 mortgage, they didn't think a couple of 30-day late payments on their two maxed-out Visa cards and one 60-day late payment on their mortgage would cause a serious problem. But, when their lender called asking about a two-year-old medical collection account they had forgotten about, the situation started to look grim.

Leon and Tamee told the lender they thought the insurance company was supposed to pay the bill. However, they had never taken the time to follow up and had ignored several statements from the clinic. After about four months, the clinic sent the account to a collection agency, which reported to the credit bureau. Now Leon and Tamee's credit score took a bigger hit.

With a credit score around 600, the lender felt she could still put a loan together, but Leon and Tamee would have to pay off the collection account first. They would also need at least 20 percent down, pay an interest rate one percent higher than the current market rate, plus pay 2 discount points.

In real dollars-and-cents terms, their low credit score will cost Leon and Tamee 2 discount points or $4,600, and the higher rate will cost them an extra $104 a month, or $3,744 over three years. Hopefully, they can get their credit cleared up and refinance to a lower interest rate by then.

The bottom line is that a credit score determines how much the mortgage will cost in interest and closing costs. In Leon and Tamee's case, not taking their credit seriously would have cost them a minimum of $8,344 in penalties and put them into sub-prime loan country where interest rates and closing costs are higher. Unfortunately, once they found out what their costs would be they had to cancel plans to sell their small bungalow and buy the new two-story they wanted.

With Sub-Primes, It's Buyer Beware

If your score is under 600, your only option may be a sub-prime mortgage. With sub-primes it's the Wild West, so you definitely want to read the fine print. Because these loan programs often have predatory prepayment penalties and inflated terms, you may want to take a year or two to repair your credit before selling your home and moving up.

One couple, Joshua and Stacie, put their home on the market and a week later signed a purchase agreement with a 30-day closing. With the sale of their home out of the way, they went house shopping and found a larger home in the same school district that was FSBO. It was exactly what they were looking for, so they made an offer—subject to their home closing—and their offer was accepted.

Then, almost as an afterthought, Joshua and Stacie decided they had better get busy and find a mortgage lender. Stacie called a lender recommended by a friend in her office and set up an appointment.

When the lender pulled their credit, he found they had accrued fourteen late payments in the last two years on their mortgage loan and maxed out two credit cards. With a low 600s credit score, Joshua and Stacie could only qualify for a B loan at 2 percent over par. Even worse, closing fees would now cost them nearly 8 percent of the loan, almost double the norm. And although the lender agreed to add these fees to the loan, it made the monthly payments even higher. With the pressure on because the sale of their home was less than a month away, they decided to go ahead with the loan.

After a year of making all their payments promptly and paying down much of their debt, Joshua and Stacie went in to refinance for a lower rate. They were shocked when they were told that it would cost them nearly $4,000 in prepayment penalties to refinance. Their loan documents had a clause that if the loan was paid off within three years it would cost 4 percent of the loan balance in penalties.

This left the homeowners with few options; all they could do was stick with the high interest loan for two more years.

So, with the clarity of 20/20 hindsight, what did Joshua and Stacie do that cost them thousands of dollars?

1. They didn't look at their credit worthiness before they put their home on the market.

2. They sold their home and made an offer on another home before they even contacted a lender.

3. There was no shopping around for the best mortgage lender or comparing loan programs. They went with the first lender they talked to.

4. Because they put themselves in a pressure situation, they ended up with a B loan from an unscrupulous lender. This cost them thousands of dollars more in closing fees, a higher interest rate, and a prepayment penalty that delayed refinancing for two years.

It's obvious in this case that Joshua and Stacie would have been much further ahead by cleaning up their credit before moving up. How could they have gone about repairing their credit?

All About Credit Repair

When a mortgage lender pulls your credit and finds a few problems that can slow you down getting into your next home, here are some things you can do:

■ Beware of credit scams where operators promise to "fix" your credit for a few hundred dollars. Unfortunately, there are no quick fixes, magic potions, or silver bullets that will transform a credit rating from bad to good. It's better to spend the money paying down a credit card than buying into a credit fixing scam that in the end won't improve your credit.

■ Pay down debt on high-interest credit cards as much as possible. Getting your balances down to under one-half the limit is best.

■ Pay off and close out small, seldom-used accounts. Too much credit can be a negative.

■ Limit the number of inquiries on your credit. A flurry of credit checks can raise a red flag and cost you points.

■ Of course, the best credit builder is making your payments on time. Late payments of 30 days or more are guaranteed to slash points from your FICO score.

■ Your payment history the past two years carries the most weight. Prior problems, such as a bankruptcy, have less or no impact after two years if you clearly show you've cleaned up your act.

■ Work with a reputable mortgage lender. Most lenders will be glad to go over your credit and work up a list of areas you can improve

Credit Score Reducing Traps

- ■ Avoid preapproved credit-card applications or extended financing offers until after you close.

- ■ Close accounts that you don't use. Mortgage lenders don't like to see lots of open accounts.

- ■ Avoid switching insurance companies or refinancing, these often bring on new inquiries.

or identify problems that need to be corrected. They know the credit system and what it takes to get you qualified for the best mortgage rates.

Definitely, don't follow Clay and Jackie's example. When their lender told them with their 720 credit score and stable job history they wouldn't have a problem qualifying for the new home they wanted, they went shopping.

Excited by the news, they opened a Home Depot and two local furniture store accounts and bought furniture and appliances. And feeling they were smart shoppers, they put their purchases on all three stores' 90-days-free-interest plans.

A few days later when the mortgage lender updated Clay and Jackie's credit report before submitting to underwriting, she was shocked to find their FICO score had dropped to 613. The lender had counseled them to avoid any credit applications or transactions until they closed on their mortgage.

But in the excitement of furnishing a new home, Clay and Jackie got carried away. This killed the deal on the new home but not the one they were living in. When they tried to back out of the sale, the buyers threatened to sue. Rather than create a messy situation, Clay and Jackie moved into an apartment. If all goes well, they should be able to buy another home in about a year.

After you've made sure your credit is in good shape, the next step is to pull all the numbers together.

By the Numbers, How Much Can You Qualify For?

With a good estimate of what you'll net when your home closes, the next step is to determine what you'll qualify for. If you're going with a large down payment, you'll likely be looking for an 80-percent LTV (loan-to-value) or less mortgage, where you don't have to pay PMI (private mortgage insurance). With 20 percent or more down payment, qualifying is a little easier than if you are a first-time home buyer with a minimum down.

Although each lender can have a slightly different focus, most like to keep income-to-debt ratios close to the following numbers. Keep in mind that these ratios are credit driven, meaning that the better your credit and the more down payment you have, the higher your debt-to-income can be.

■ Typically, total debt *plus* the mortgage payment—with principal, interest, taxes, and insurance included (PITI)—shouldn't exceed 40 percent of your income before taxes. Although, in some instances where the borrower has exceptional assets, a high credit score, and/or other pluses, this ratio can go to 50 percent or higher.

■ Total house payment (PITI) shouldn't exceed 31 percent of gross monthly income. For second-time home buyers, however, this ratio can be stretched with good credit, a larger down payment, and stable work history.

For example, when Colby and Marie decided to sell their home and move up to a newer home, they sat down and looked at their pay stubs for the last couple of months. Their combined income totaled $7,240 a month before deductions. Their monthly payments—$545 for a car payment, $150 Visa card, $75 Discover card, and a $190 student loan—totaled $960.

Because of Colby and Marie's good credit score, job history, and their ability to pay 25 percent down from the sale of their previous home, their mortgage lender told them they could borrow up to 46 percent of their income minus their debts. Which in this case would be $2,888 a month.

Monthly taxes and insurance are obtained by adding the yearly premiums and then dividing by 12 months. (Property taxes vary considerably from state to state, so call your county assessor for data on your area.) A good rule of thumb is to figure that taxes and insurance make up 20 percent of the payment. In this case it would be $2,888 × .20 = $578, and subtracting that from $2,888 would leave $2,310 for the principal and interest part of the payment. Using a financial calculator and keying in a pay-

Financial Calculators
You can buy inexpensive financial calculators from Staples, Office Max, Office Depot, etc. Calculated Industries has an excellent line you can order online at: *www.calculated.com.* Most of the mortgage lender Internet sites—such as *www .mortgagexpo.com*—have financial calculators. Also, you can download software from *www.template zone.com.* If you have a palm pilot, check out *www .palmgear.com.*

ment of $2,310, 6.5 percent interest, and 30 years (360 months) gives $365,467 as the maximum loan amount. Since Colby and Marie are putting 25 percent down or $121,822, that amount is added to the loan amount to get $487,289 as the maximum home price they can write an offer on.

In a way, the system is rigged for second-time-plus home buyers. If you've kept your credit clean and built some equity to use for a down payment, you get a better interest rate, no PMI payments, and higher qualifying ratios.

Counting Income from a Second Job

Income from a second job may or may not help the amount you can qualify for. If you've been on the second job for less than a year, many lenders won't count it. Also, part-time sales income and other sources that can't be verified on your tax return stand only a slim chance of helping your ratios.

Monthly payments from child support and other verifiable income streams can usually be counted especially if they show up on your tax return.

If you need to include income from child support, you'll need to give the lender a copy of the divorce decree and bank statements, showing the money is coming in monthly.

In one particular sale, a buyer had sold a rental home a couple of years ago and carried the financing. Although the monthly cash flow coming in was less than $200, he reported the income on his federal tax return and could show the lender a paper trail. It made the difference in qualifying for the loan.

In another instance, a mortgage applicant was tending several small children in her home. She couldn't document the cash flow from tax records, so the lender wasn't able to credit the income on the application. The key is being able to prove to the lender that the income is consistent and long term, from tax records or bank statements.

Earlier it was suggested that you work from a conservative Good Faith Estimate so you have a reserve in case you need to sweeten the pot to attract a buyer in a slow market. The next section maps out how you can use points to do this.

Points and Buydowns 101

Randall and Tanya were upset because their home had been on the market for two months and only three couples showed enough interest to walk through. Clearly, they needed to do something differently, options were running out, and the possibility of losing their home hung over them like a black thundercloud.

It was a slow market and there were several similar homes for sale in the area that had been on the market about as long. Randall and Tanya were getting discouraged and they decided to lower their price; if that didn't work, they would do a deed in lieu of foreclosure—a move that would give the home back to the bank, but wipe out their credit and the equity they had built up.

Their agent suggested that instead of lowering their price in hopes of getting more action, they offer to pay points and advertise a lower-than-par interest rate. Here's how that works:

When you call a mortgage banker about a home loan, it's likely the lender will reel off a whole smorgasbord of interest rates. In addition to the current or par rate, the lender will also give you the choice of several lower rates if you're willing to buy down the interest rate or pay "points." By paying points and getting a lower interest rate, you create a great selling tool.

The agent and sellers changed the game plan and offered buyers a two-one buydown. With this type of program, borrowers get a 2 percent lower rate the first year and a 1 percent lower rate the second year. That meant the sellers could advertise—on their fliers and ads—a beginning interest rate 2 percent less than the going rate.

It wasn't long before buyers attracted by the flier's teaser headlines started coming through the home, and two weeks later a couple made an offer.

If your market is a little slow also, the next section explains how you can make points work for you in attracting a buyer.

How Points and Buydowns Work

A point is one percent of the loan amount and is interest paid up front to increase the investor's yield or profit on the loan. For example, if you call a mortgage lender for the current rate you might get 6.0 percent at par, or 5.75 percent if you'll pay a point. On a $100,000 loan this would add $1,000 to your closing costs to buy the interest down for the life of the loan.

However, since few mortgages go full term anymore because of sale or refinance, points can be an attractive incentive for investors to invest in these mortgages.

As a rule-of-thumb, each point reduces the interest rate by about $1/4$ percent on a 30-year mortgage. However, it's a competitive market so you should shop around for the best point/rate combo. Rates can and do change daily, and in a volatile market, they change several times a day.

You usually have two choices when you play with mortgage interest rates: One, you can lock in the interest rate and points for thirty to sixty days. Or two, you can float and take whatever the market is the day you close. If you like to gamble and the rates are falling, this can be a good way to go. But, if you don't want to take the chance of getting caught by an upward spurt in interest rates, then locking the rate is the safe bet.

When a builder or seller offers to pay the bank a point or more to lower an interest rate, it's called a buydown. Often builders increase the price of the home so they can advertise an attractive interest rate. As a consumer, you should ask the lender or salesperson how many points are built into the price of financing when the interest quote is lower than the current rate. There's no free lunch in mortgages. If you encounter an interest rate less than the current rate, someone is picking up the difference, and that's usually you, so beware!

Buydown programs are varied and limited only by the lender's imagination. Although permanent buydowns are the most common, two-one temporary programs are a close runner up. Buydowns are also a great sales tool, and how to use them to sell your home in a slow market is covered next.

Using Buydowns as a Selling Tool

As mentioned earlier, many home sellers are tempted to lower the price to make their home more competitive. But, an effective alternative is decide how much money you're willing to spend in lowering the price and see how far it will go buying down the interest rate.

A good rule-of-thumb for figuring how much a two-one buydown will cost you is multiply the loan amount by .02625. For example, a $160,000 loan times .02625 will cost about $4,200.

To do this, first find out from mortgage lenders in your area how far the money you've allocated will lower the interest rate. For example, suppose you've decided to spend $3,000 to help attract a buyer. A mortgage lender tells you the current rate is 6.00 percent and he will go $\frac{1}{4}$ of a percent per point. If the loan amount is $150,000, then your $3,000 investment will lower the buyer's interest rate from 6.00 to 5.50 percent and help your buyers qualify for the mortgage.

In fact, this is exactly the route Randall and Tanya took to energize their home-selling campaign. They decided to pay up to $3,000 to buy down the rate rather than lower the price. Their agent redid the fliers and ran ads highlighting a special financing option with a rate ½ percent lower than par.

Interest in the home and showings picked up with the special financing promotion, and it wasn't long before an offer came in from a couple who had been looking in a slightly lower price range. When they saw how the buydown rate would make it possible for them to qualify for more house, they went for it.

To illustrate how the numbers work, suppose you have a buyer who can't quite qualify to buy your $160,000 home. Rather than lower the price you agree to pay points so the buyers can qualify. The buyers in this case are going with a zero-down loan and paying their own closing costs.

The loan is for $160,000 at 6.75 percent interest and 30 years. Normal monthly payment is $1,037.76, which the buyer can't quite qualify for. However, you agree to pay $4,200 to buy the rate down so they can qualify with a two-one buydown.

As you can see in Figure 6-1, qualifying on the first- or second-year payment can make a difference, and you're paying a concession to make the sale work. On the other hand, if you had just reduced the price, you wouldn't have gained much. Buyers would likely still come in lower than your asking price.

Although points and buydowns are great when the seller picks up the tab, how good a deal are they when you have to write the check when you're buying a home?

Is It Worth Paying Points When You Buy Your Next Home?

Whether it's worth paying points depends on how long you're going to be in the house. If you plan on staying in the home for a few years

FIGURE 6-1 Two-one buydown payment schedule ($160,000 loan, 6.75 percent interest).	
First-Year Payment (4.75 Percent)	$ 834.64
Second-Year Payment (5.75 Percent)	$ 933.72
Third-Year Payment (6.75 Percent Thereafter)	$1,037.76

then points can save you money. To determine how much you'll save, subtract the payment if you buy down the rate from the payment if you don't. Divide this difference into what the points will cost.

For example, on a $100,000 loan at 6 percent for 30 years, the monthly payment is $599.55. But, if you pay $1,000 to buy the rate down to 5.75 percent, the payment is $583.57, a difference of $15.98 a month. Dividing the $15.98 monthly savings into the $1,000 points cost means it will be about 63 months (five years plus) before you start saving $15.98 a month.

This is hardly a barn-burner investment. True, an accountant could fine-tune the numbers by factoring in tax angles and payoffs, but in the end, how long you keep the home is still the most important factor. Keeping the home for thirty years would save you roughly $5,000. However, most financial advisors don't recommend going beyond three to four years to recoup your point costs.

Mathematically, the higher the interest rate the better deal points become. If mortgage rates were to soar to 10 percent or more, buydowns and paying points would become more important in mortgage decisions.

Keep in mind that interest rates and points can change daily, but you can lock in the rates for 30 to 60 days until you're ready to close. However, 30-day locks usually have better terms than 60-day locks. Always shop around for the best deal. A summary of how points and buydowns work is shown in Figure 6-2.

As you can see, points can be used to buy your mortgage down when you *buy* a home, and to create a selling tool when you *sell*, especially in a difficult market.

Another important and expensive but less visible part of the selling process is title insurance. Most sellers don't think about it until they arrive at the title company to sign the closing paperwork. The importance of title insurance to your sale is discussed next.

Title Insurance 101

In many states the purpose of the title company is three-fold: they sell title insurance, they handle escrow funds, and they do the actual closing where you go in and sign the paperwork. In other states it is attorneys or escrow companies that do the actual closing. But, regardless of who does the closing, title companies still provide the title insurance coverage on your property.

FIGURE 6-2
Summary of points and buydowns.

Program	Details
Permanent Buydowns	Each point equals 1 percent of the loan amount and lowers the interest rate 1/8 to 1/4 of a percent for the life of the loan. This helps you qualify for a higher mortgage and save on the monthly payment if you keep the loan for a long period.
Temporary Buydowns	Two-one buydowns reduce the interest rate 2 percent the first year and 1 percent the second. These programs are especially helpful for first-time home buyers or those whose income is increasing.
Using Points as a Sales Tool	By paying points for the buyer you can buy down their interest rate and make your sale more competitive. Builders often use this technique so they can advertise lower rates.
Paying Points to Lower Your Rate	Divide the savings from paying points into the cost of the points to find out how long it takes to recoup the cost. If payback goes beyond 48 months, it may not be worth it.

Title insurance is one of the biggest yet least understood costs in selling a home. It's one of those fees that you don't get involved in directly.

For most people, a title policy is just part of the closing paperwork, and they never give it a second thought. But, as is true of homeowner's insurance: When you need it, you really need it. This is because title problems, property boundaries, deed forgeries, and unreleased liens can pop up and cause huge, expensive problems over a home you've sold—even years later.

In one example, buyers thought they had bought a home on 3/4 of an acre that backed up to a county park. What the seller forgot to tell them was that six months' earlier the county had bought an easement for a joggers' trail where their property connected to the park. This reduced the back property line by 20 feet; somehow the title company had missed the easement in their title search. When the new buyers were landscaping their backyard, a surveyor party came by, staking out the jogging trail, and told them they were encroaching on county property. Understandably, the new homeowners were upset and called the title company. Luckily, the title policy the sellers had paid for at closing was with a good company and they settled with the buyers.

What would have happened if there had been no title policy? Right, chances are good that if you sold the property without disclosing or knowing about the easement you would get to see the nice wood paneling inside a courtroom along with sizeable attorney's fees.

For more information on title insurance, check out the following Web sites:

www.alta.org

www.firstam.com

www.landam.com/ home.htm

In another example, Paul and Linda bought an older home in a small town, and the tax notice described the property dimensions as 110 feet × 140 feet. That had been the accepted dimensions for 75 years and for the previous six buyers.

The new buyers decided to put up a fence. When they measured 110 feet from the east corner they found their lot went about 7 feet into their neighbor's living room—a potentially messy situation.

Paul and Linda contacted the title company that insured their sale and they had a surveyor check out the property corners. As it turned out, the old town survey had a few problems. All the lot lines along the street now had to be readjusted and new property descriptions had to be worked up and recorded in the county recorder's office. It turned into a several-thousand-dollar project, which the title company paid for. Again, had the sellers not paid for a good title policy, they would likely have faced expensive litigation.

All About the Seller's Policy

One of the biggest closing costs is the title insurance. In most states this is how you guarantee good and marketable title, so you don't have much choice if you want to sell. Title insurance costs vary from state to state. Some states set the rates, others require that insurers file their rates with their state department of insurance, and some don't regulate the fees.

In Iowa, for example, home buyers typically purchase a title-warranty certificate from the Iowa Finance Authority. You get the same coverage as title insurance at a fraction of the cost. Your Realtor or a mortgage lender can tell you what the norm is in your state.

Regardless of what state you're in, you'll find the title insurance costs on line 1108 of the HUDs, which are discussed in the next section on closing costs and how to read closing statements.

All About Closing and Selling Costs

Just as you had a mountain of paperwork to sign when you bought your home, you get to revisit the mountain when you sell. This time, it's smaller and more straightforward, but you still have to be vigilant to avoid paying more than you have to. This section will cover your selling costs and how they're represented on the paperwork, so your eyes don't glaze over when the forms are shoved across the table for you to sign.

How to Read the HUD Settlement Statements

All closings involving a mortgage company, bank, or other financial entity are detailed on $8^{1/2}$ inch $\times$ 14 inch legal size HUD-1 Settlement Statement forms, known as the HUDs. The upper part of page one has the names and addresses of the buyers, sellers, closer, and mortgage lender. The rest of the form is divided into two columns: The left column (Section J) is labeled Summary of Borrower's Transaction; the right column (Section K) is labeled Summary of Seller's Transaction.

Since you're the seller, the columns reproduced below are for your side of the transaction, or Section K, only. The lines are numbered from 400 at the top to 603 at the bottom, where you discover how much money you walk away with.

Suppose, for example, that you sold your home for $400,000 and were going over the HUDs at closing. The first section you would look at are the lines numbered in the 400s, Gross Amount Due to Seller. This is the sales price plus any credits you have coming, like personal property you're selling the buyers, taxes you've paid in advance, or assessments (if you live in a condo or townhouse) that the buyer is reimbursing you. In this case lines 405 to 419 are blank since there were no more items to add to the sales price.

K. Summary of Seller's Transaction	
400. Gross Amount Due to Seller	
401. Contract Sale Price	400,000.00
402. Personal Property (refrigerator)	475.00

Adjustment for items paid by seller in advance	
403. City/town taxes	278.00
404. County taxes	63.00
420. Gross Amount Due To Seller	400,816.00

The next section is the 500 numbered entries. Where the 400 numbers give you money, the 500 numbers take it away. This section lists all the totals from page 2 (where all the charges are broken down item by item) that are subtracted from your gross sales price (line 420 above).

500. Reductions in Amount Due Seller	
501. Excess deposits	-0-
502. Settlement charges (line 1400, page 2)	26,200.00
503. Payoff of first mortgage to Arcadia National Bank	287,642.00
504. Payoff of Key Bank equity credit line	9,563.00
505. Roof repairs payment to Horizon Roofing Co.	2,354.00
506. Earnest money held by XYZ Realty	2,500.00
Adjustments for items unpaid by seller	
507. County taxes 01/01/04 to 07/13/04 @ $3,890 year	2,409.64
520. Total Reduction Amount Due Seller	330,668.64
601. Gross amount due Seller (line 420)	400,816.00
602. Less reductions to amounts due to Seller (line 520)	330,668.64
603. Cash (X to) (from) Seller	70,147.36

Line 507 refers to your county/property tax. How these are collected varies. In the example above it's yearly, and the seller is responsible for taxes from January 1st to closing day. If taxes are paid quarterly, they are prorated from the start of the second quarter, or July 1, to closing day. In this case the seller would owe for 13 days.

Line 603 is the bottom line. In this case, the "cash to" box is checked, meaning you'll get a check from the closing agent for $70,147.36. If you had sold for a loss, the "cash from" box would be checked and you would feel the pain of writing a check to the closing agent.

The 700-numbered entries on page 2 of the settlement statement break down the commission and related costs. This page has three columns. The first one describes the item or charge, the second column shows buyer's costs, and the third column shows seller's costs. The sample below shows the seller's column only.

Lines 700 to 704 are commissions paid to a real estate company for selling your home. You'll want to run a quick check and make sure the percentage you agreed to is correct and that no other charges have been added to your column, especially in the Supplemental Summary line 704.

L. Settlement Charges	
700. Total sales/broker's commission based on price $400,000 @ 6.00% = $24,000	Paid from Seller's Funds at Settlement
703. Total commission paid at settlement to XYZ Reality	$24,000.00
704. Supplemental summary	-0-

The 800, 900, and 1000 numbered lines list items payable in connection with the loan. These are buyer's costs. Unless you agreed to pay some of their costs as sales concessions you won't have any entries in your (seller's) column.

When you get about midway down the form to lines numbered 1100 to 1117, charges will start appearing in the seller's column again. These are title and closing fees, which both buyers and sellers will have in their respective columns. Each state handles title and closing fees differently, and the person closing the loan will go over what charges are standard for your area. In other words, there's going to be a bunch of small fees in the 1100 section.

1100. Title Charges	
1101. Settlement or closing fee to First American Title Insurance Agency, LLC	130.00
1102. Abstract or title search	
1103. Title examination	
1104. Title insurance binder	
1105. Document fee	

1106. Notary fee	
1107. Attorney fee	
1108. Title insurance to First American Title Insurance Agency, LLC	1,800.00
1112. Document preparation fee to First American Title Insurance Agency, LLC	150.00
1113. Overnight delivery to First American Title Insurance Agency, LLC	30.00
1114. Reconveyance fee	90.00

Lines 1200 to 1206 deal with government recording and transfer charges. If your state, county, or city has real-estate transfer taxes, these will appear on this section.

Lines 1300 to 1314 are miscellaneous or additional settlement charges. Pay close attention to this section to make sure that buyer's costs, such as survey or pest inspections, are not charged to you unless you've agreed to it.

Finally, the last line, 1400, totals all the costs on page 2 and the total is entered on line 502, page 1 as discussed previously.

1400. Total Settlement Charges (enter on lines 103, Section J and 502, Section K)	26,200

At the Closing Table with Pen in Hand

You should now be comfortable with the HUDs, or at least not find them so intimidating. When the closing agent slides them across the table for your signature, take a moment to go over the sections. Make sure the mortgage company hasn't inadvertently put some buyer fees in the seller's 800 column.

Suppose, for example, that you've agreed to pay $3,200 in concessions, you'll want to make sure the costs on Sellers Credit line 506 doesn't exceed this amount.

Also, how the closing agents go over these numbers at closing can vary. Some start out on page 2, go over the different fees, then flip to page 1 and show you

Because some costs are favorite places for lenders and title companies to pad the fees, you'll want to look closely at the following:

- Tax service fee: A fee to verify the property taxes are current ($30 to $50).
- Underwriter fee: If there is one, it should be a buyer's fee.

where the totals go. Others will do the opposite and go over the big picture on page 1 before going to page 2 for the details.

After you sign the paperwork, the package will go to the lender. Upon receipt of funds—usually within a day or two—the title company will record the transaction, and your proceeds will be available to be picked up or transferred electronically into your account.

If you've purchased another home, hopefully that stack of paperwork—much higher this time—is making it all worthwhile.

In the unhappy event your home isn't selling as hoped and the *For Sale* sign in the lawn isn't quite as vertical, the next chapter will give you some ideas on how to pump up your marketing.

- **Administrative fee: A** typical garbage fee.
- **Processing fee: Some** lenders and real estate companies are adding a $250 processing fee. Don't let them get away with it.
- **Assignment fee: Not a** seller's cost.
- **Flood certification fee:** Normally a buyer's fee.
- **Recording fees: Make** sure you're not charged more than it costs to record your releases on your mortgages with the county.
- **Courier fee: Question this** one and whether a courier is actually needed or used.
- **Document prep: Look** closely at document prep fees.

CHAPTER 7

Extreme Marketing: Alternatives to Selling

In hot markets like San Francisco, Boston, New York, and other similar areas, information on what to do when a house isn't selling may not seem relevant. It's important to keep in mind though that markets can change in a day from hot to glacial. Pending sales can evaporate and closings postponed or canceled.

A good example of this was in the early 1980s: Inflation was running hot, the economy was reeling, and mortgage interest rates jumped to 16 percent almost overnight. In real estate offices across the country, big white sales boards displaying pending sales were wiped clean as buyers could no longer qualify and deals fell apart.

But interestingly, it wasn't too long before new sales started appearing back on office sales boards. Agents, buyers, and sellers found ways to put deals together despite the economy. People still needed to buy and sell homes; real estate is a basic commodity, and that hasn't changed.

And that's the purpose of this chapter. Not doom and gloom, but to explore different ways and options you can use if your home isn't selling or the market value is less than your mortgage balance. In areas with normal or slow markets, having a few alternate options can avert a financial crisis if a home doesn't sell or if the home has depreciated so much that market value is less than the remaining mortgage.

The first section of the chapter will look at some of the things you can do in a slow market to move your home-selling project into the fast lane.

Days-on-Market Averages Can Be Deceiving

If 50 percent of the home buyers in your area suddenly stopped buying, you would still have the other 50 percent buying homes. Homes are a basic commodity, and you can either rent or buy. Fortunately for the real estate industry, the pressure on most people is to live the American dream, and that means owning your own home as soon as possible. If you look at the glass as being half full, out of a possible 100 buyers, you would have 50 people buying homes.

In such markets, if you were to look on the MLS at the average days-on-market (DOM), you might see that the average selling time is 79 days. But, if you look closely you'll find many homes are selling in less than 30 days. So, what do these homes have that others don't?

- Homes are likely to be in desirable established neighborhoods close to shopping, universities, good schools, and medical centers. As these areas become more upscale and trendy, they tend to resist market ups and downs.

- They are in good condition, have curb appeal, and have no deferred maintenance.

- Prices are carefully researched and are in line with neighborhood values.

- Sellers are flexible on financing terms if needed.

- Marketing reaches people who are likely to buy in the area.

You may not be able to change the area you live in, but you still have more control than you think over getting your home sold in a slow market. If you doubt this, have your Realtor pull up the homes for sale in your area and you go see them. Pretend you're a buyer, and you'll be amazed when you go through these homes how few you can get excited about.

What If You're Not in the Best Area?

The toughest problem to solve in selling a home is area. As the saying goes, you can remodel, tear down, or paint, but you can't move the location. If you find you're in a challenged area you may consider the following:

- You're probably not going to attract buyers looking for their dream home, but you can appeal to buyers looking for an investment or a first-time home buyer who has little cash. Perhaps you can pay their down payment and closing costs. Yes, it's going to cost you, but this approach can be less expensive than selling to a bargain hunter.

■ If the home needs work, paint and cleanup can work wonders and make a home more attractive to first-time buyers who are short on cash. You can advertise for these types of buyers by running no-money-down ads in your local daily or weekly paper.

■ Consider keeping the home as a rental. Many times an area goes up in value as conditions change. One investor, for example, bought several homes in a not-so-good area and rented them for twelve years. Eventually, new subdivisions went in nearby and area land values went into low orbit. His home's values went up too and he sold out for a big profit.

What If Condition Is a Problem

In an overheated market when values are spiraling up, you can play fast and loose with upgrades and get away with it. No matter what you do seems to increase the home's value. But, unfortunately, the economy changes and hot markets cool, so you have to be more careful choosing which upgrades you want to make.

Earlier chapters discussed upgrading to make a house more saleable, but if you don't have a lot of equity, you'll need to do some extreme cost analysis before rehabing. This is where the cost of every nail and brush stroke is measured against the projected sales price.

In Salt Lake City, John and Judy Morrill buy and fix up homes for a living. For twenty-five years they've maximized profits by making homes look good while keeping costs low. They are masters of extreme rehabbing. Here are their suggestions for how you can make your house more saleable:

■ If the kitchen is dated or the worse for wear, you can paint the cabinets a gloss white, or sand and stain them, rather than replace them. If you need to replace them consider:

1. Discontinued styles at home centers and cabinet shops.

2. Look for damaged cabinets that when installed won't show the damage.

3. Check out demolition yards in the yellow pages. It's amazing what you can get for little cost.

4. Call remodeling contractors. They may have kitchen remodels where the owners will sell their old cabinets cheap. Homeown-

ers sometimes replace perfectly good cabinets because they want to upgrade to the latest finish or style.

5. Check local classified ads, eBay, or run your own ad to find what you're looking for.

■ Dated counters can be replaced with laminate rather than more expensive materials. Check at counter shops for discontinued patterns, returns, and laminate roll ends. With so many edge-finishing options possible—such as wood, tile, and metal—you can make counters look great without a big expense.

■ Try having a professional clean our carpets before replacing them, if they are not too worn. If you have to replace them, shop for special sales, mill ends, and discontinued patterns or styles.

■ Take extra care with any painting you do and make it look as professional as possible because this is a high visibility item. Paint the trim and wall contrasting colors and carry the color scheme from room to room.

■ You can often cut painting costs by checking at paint stores for five-gallon returns that are slightly off tint.

■ Clean up the yard and trim shrubbery and trees; it can make a big difference in outside appeal.

■ Of course, making the house exterior as appealing as possible is important too. A good cleaning or paint job can make it a different house.

How One Couple Did It

Phil and Sherry had to go the extreme marketing route when they had to sell their home in a slow market and without much equity. There were three homes already for sale on their street, which had been on the market for over a month.

Phil's job transfer was coming up in 60 days and he didn't want to leave Sherry alone to handle selling the house and moving with their four-year-old twin girls. Their home, a 1980s bilevel, was in good condition but dated. The dark cabinets, orange laminate counters, and patterned flooring definitely discouraged buyers from imagining themselves living there. Clearly, something was needed.

The sellers set up a meeting with their agent and worked up a list of improvements that would make their house more competitive yet not cost a lot.

Here's what they did:

- Since the cabinets were in good shape, the sellers elected to paint the cabinets a gloss white. It was a messy job—painting and sanding between coats—but the result was outstanding. With new hardware replacing the old hinges and door pulls, the total cost was around $300.

- Shopping around, the sellers were able to find a section of vinyl flooring in a discontinued light-colored pattern for the kitchen and bath at a local home improvement store. Adding in the cost for installation, the total costs came to slightly less than $500.

- Next came the interior paint. The old paint wasn't in good condition, so the owners decided to paint all the rooms a champagne color with bright white trim. It took three days of hard work but the result was worth it. Total cost was about $250 for paint and supplies.

When all was done the inside was transformed. It appeared larger and brighter with the fresh paint. It was something buyers could now get excited about.

The exterior was brick and vinyl siding, so Phil rented a pressure sprayer for two hours. After cutting through layers of grime, the exterior looked almost new again. The $80 rental cost turned out to be a great investment.

Fortunately, the roof and landscaping were in good shape, so a dose of nitrogen-rich fertilizer (about $60) and a good watering regimen got the lawn headed toward a lush green. Total costs were about $1,200 and many hours of sweat and work. It was worth it—there was now hope.

And that hope blossomed about two weeks later when a cooperating agent on the MLS showed a young couple through who made an offer. Phil and Sherry's agent had replaced the photos and reworded the remarks on the MLS listing. This resulted in an agent adding the home to a short list she was putting together to show her clients. If the redecorating had not happened, the agent would most likely not have included the home on the list. Her clients were young first-time home buyers who didn't want to handle anything more than moving in.

Sweetening the Pot with Assumptions and Lease-Options

If you are having trouble selling, you might consider making your home more attractive to a different kind of buyer—one who typically doesn't qualify for financing. With the hundreds of mortgage plans and liberal credit requirements available, most buyers *can* qualify for financing. There are several situations, however, where letting the buyers take on your loan or working out a lease-option may make sense. Before offering this kind of deal, make sure your loan is assumable.

Not All Loans Are Assumable

Normally, FHA and VA loans can be assumed at the note interest rate if the buyers can qualify under the usual guidelines. For example, if you have an FHA loan at $5\frac{1}{2}$ percent and the current rate is 7 percent, a buyer can assume your loan at the lower rate. They'll have to pay an assumption fee (typically $500 plus credit check fee) and qualify on credit and income. If they have the money to cash out your equity, the buyers can get a good deal.

Veterans Affairs (VA) loans are more difficult. Veterans can only assume the loan if they have eligibility and can qualify. But, as with FHA loans, they can end up with a less-than-the-going-rate mortgage.

How you handle your equity is between you and the borrower. For example, if you have a buyer for your home willing to pay $180,000, and you owe $160,000, your equity is $20,000. You can have the buyer pay your equity in cash, or part cash and part note. Or you can take a boat, car, snowmobile, Harley motorcycle, or whatever. In real estate speak, this is called creative financing.

As interest rates go up in the future more of these deals are likely to happen, as homeowners with FHA mortgages find they can use their lower rates as a marketing tool.

As for conventional Fannie Mae and

What Does "Assume a Loan" Mean?

A buyer can assume someone's mortgage only with the permission of the lender and must qualify on income and credit for the loan balance.

If the loan has a lower interest rate than the current rate and the lender will let you keep it, it's a good way to go.

When buyers qualify to assume the loan, the lender releases the sellers so they are no longer liable.

Freddie Mac loans, you're out of luck. They're nonassumable and due on sale.

A word of caution here, many real estate scams involve people trying to get around due-on-sale clauses illegally. Usually they'll create a new trust deed (mortgage) that incorporates the existing one the bank has recorded along with a few paragraphs outlining how the buyer is going to pay the seller for their equity. This is called a wrap-around or all-inclusive trust deed. The scam part comes about because the seller is conveying (selling) an interest in the property in violation of the mortgage terms. If the lender finds out about it, they will likely foreclose on the loan.

Even though there are all sorts of schemes out there touted by so-called creative financing gurus, be careful to avoid crossing the line into fraud and losing big bucks.

In one case, a couple who had gotten a transfer and couldn't sell their home talked to an investor/agent. When he stopped by, he told them he would be willing to buy their home with $1,000 down and the balance of their equity due in one year with interest. The investor went on to explain that they could sell using a wrap-around trust deed without triggering the bank's due-on-sale clause. It sounded like a solution to a sticky problem, so the sellers agreed.

Several months later the sellers got a late notice from the lender that a payment hadn't come in. They didn't worry about it too much until they got a letter telling them they were two months behind. Another two weeks went by when they received a certified letter telling them that they had defaulted on their note by selling the property. The letter also spelled out that due to the default the entire loan balance plus late fees was due and payable.

Long story short, the sellers couldn't come up with the money to pay off the loan, and the house went into foreclosure. The investor had rented the property and after a couple of payments started pocketing the rents knowing it would take the bank several months to go through a default sale.

As for the sellers, the default ruined their credit for several years and wiped out any equity they had in the property.

Another option, lease-options can be a better way to go if you're careful and follow a few common sense rules.

Lease-Options: Tread Carefully

If, in spite of your best efforts, your home doesn't sell and you've got to move to another town, a lease-option can be a good way to go short term. Still, there are pros and cons to consider.

Lease-option downsides are:

■ In reality you've got a tenant who may or may not take care of the home. If they fulfill the terms of the agreement and buy the home, no problem. But if they can't, move out, and leave the house a mess, you'll end up spending hefty bucks to fix it up. In other words, you're gambling that the people you lease to can or will perform down the road.

■ If you're out of state, you'll need someone local to be your eyes and ears to make sure all is well with your house. This can be friends, relatives, or a professional rental agency. Rental agencies typically charge 10 to 15 percent of the monthly rent.

■ When the time comes for the lessees to perform and they can't, you'll have some hard choices to make:

1. It's difficult to sell a home with tenants in it; they have a bad habit of pointing out all the problems to potential buyers.

2. You probably won't want to evict the tenants and lose the cash flow. A vacant home with you making the house payments is called a hungry alligator in the real estate industry.

3. In the end, the third and most painless choice is continue and rent to the tenants hoping they'll be able to get their act together in the near future.

■ Time isn't on your side. Few tenants take as good a care of a home as the owner does. The longer it rents, the more shopworn it becomes and the more you'll spend restoring it to saleable condition.

Still, there are ways to protect yourself in a lease-option, as shown in Figure 7-1.

Erik and Mandy went a lease-option route when they needed to move because of a job transfer and couldn't sell their home. Fortunately, it was a good rental market in their area, so finding someone interested in a lease-option wasn't too difficult.

The first eight months went smoothly, but then the situation went downhill when the tenants ended up getting a divorce and moved out.

The sellers had to spend their two-week vacation cleaning the house, fixing it up, and finding another tenant. This time around they didn't go the option route, but hired a rental agency to manage the property. Luckily, a year later the tenants were able to qualify and offered to buy the home.

FIGURE 7-1
How to protect yourself with a lease-option.

Item	What You Need to Do
The Paperwork	Have an attorney do the option so if the tenants don't buy, you keep deposits or accumulated purchase credits.
Verifying Home's Condition	Take lots of photos of the home and yard so if questions arise as to condition you're covered. Photos with date/time stamp are best.
Inspecting the Property	Have someone check on the property monthly. If need be, hire a property management company.
Repairs	Tenants pay for repairs and get a credit for the costs when they buy. Make sure you get copies of the receipts (no receipt, no credit).
Sales Price	Have the sales price you've agreed to in writing as part of the lease-option. Never leave it to be determined later when they exercise the option.
What Do Tenants Forfeit if They Don't Buy?	This is the tricky part, so you'll want an attorney's help making this clause airtight.
What if Tenants Move Out Suddenly?	Have a backup plan so you can get the property cleaned up and back on the market promptly.

In spite of the negatives there are positives too:

■ You can often get more money with a lease-option than with a month-to-month rental.

■ Many times you can get a better quality tenant who will take care of the house than you can with a month-to-month agreement.

■ You may be able to get an extra hundred dollars or more a month over the going rents and apply it to the down payment if they buy the home. This gives the tenants a credit they can use for the down payment or closing costs. It's also a good incentive for them to follow through on the option.

■ You'll have a good tax deduction. If the tenants decide to buy the house and you want to invest in real estate at your new location, you can do a 1031 tax-free exchange. This allows you to transfer you equity to a new property and defer paying capital gains taxes.

Sometimes you can't sell, you have to move, and you don't have any equity. Do you punt? Here are some options.

If You Owe More Than the House Is Worth

Of course, in a hot market this situation rarely happens because the house sells fast and bails out the owner. But, in a normal or slow market, owing more than the house is worth can easily happen. If you suddenly have to sell, it can get sticky fast.

How Your Mortgage Can Be More Than the House Is Worth

■ You bought a new home and there hasn't been sufficient appreciation to cover the closing costs and extras you added into the sale price. In a hot market, break-even can happen in days; in a cold market it can take years. Many times, sellers find they're competing with new homes still going up in the area. Because they have no equity for wiggle room, selling for what is owed can be tough.

■ The economic climate or other conditions in the area cause the real estate market to nose dive. Values can go down, but unfortunately, mortgage balances don't.

■ You bought in a not-so-good area and something happened to cause the area's values to go down even more, taking your home's value with them.

■ The market was hot and you bought at the top. Then interest rates went up or something happened to slow demand; values dropped, leaving you holding the bag.

■ An oldie, but goody: A homeowner adds on to a home or over-improves for the neighborhood. The improvements are financed with a second mortgage or refinance. The rationale: "We're going to live here forever!" In real estate, forever is now less than six years.

■ The home is purchased with a buyer-assist program such as Neighborhood Gold, Nehemiah, or a similar program where down payment and closing costs are added to the sales price. In these cases, it can take several years for the loan balance to equal the home's value.

■ You refinanced your mortgage for up to 125 percent of value to pay off bills or credit cards.

■ Other causes—such as death, divorce, transfer, health, and so on—can alter plans and force you to put your home on the market.

Okay, you've got to sell and can't make the payments, what do you do next?

Working with the Mortgage Lender

The first step when you find out you can't make the payments is to call your lender's customer service. It's usually an 800 or other toll free number on your monthly statement. You will be assigned a representative to work with. Lenders don't want to go the foreclosure route unless they have to.

It's important for you to contact them as quickly as possible if you see payment problems coming. Don't wait until it gets too big for a positive solution.

Both VA and HUD (FHA) have programs that work closely with homeowners heading for default. In some cases, HUD and VA will buy back the loan from the lender and work with the homeowner on a revised payment plan. You have to qualify for these plans, but it's worth it if you're having problems making payments.

If these remedies don't work another route is the short sale. It's a little messy, but can be a good solution.

About Short Sales

Short sales—also called short payoffs, compromise sales, and pre-foreclosure sales—happen when a homeowner tries to sell a home but the mortgage balance is greater than the market value.

The typical route a short sale takes is when the homeowner gets an offer that's close to market value but less than the mortgage balance. The listing and/or selling agent (or the homeowner if going FSBO) puts together a sales package that's submitted to the lender. This package should contain:

■ A copy of the filled-out and signed (by both buyer and seller) purchase agreement along with a copy of the earnest money check.

■ MLS printouts of similar homes that have sold in the last month or two as well as competitive homes that are now on the market.

- A copy of the preapproval letter from the buyer's lender.

- A financial statement—or projected HUDs done by the title company—showing how much money the lender needs to forgive so the deal will work.

This package goes to the contact person assigned to the case by the lender. Your proposal will likely go to a committee that decides on approval, rejection, or counter.

Sometimes you'll get a quick answer on your proposal, other times it can take a few weeks and several phone calls or e-mails to get results.

It's important to let your tax advisor review the HUDs or financial statement before you submit the package. You may find out the sale carries tax penalties if you have part of a loan liability forgiven.

Unfortunately, some homeowners in short-sale situations make the mistake of waiting to contact the mortgage lender after they've missed a payment or two. That puts 30- to 60-day late dings on their credit rating and makes recovery more difficult.

It's better to work with your lender before you miss a payment. Don't delay when it becomes apparent you may need to go the short-sale route.

Credit wise, a foreclosure means you have to wait three years before you can get another mortgage. Although there are B lenders who will work with you after a year, the price is steep and the terms are less than friendly.

The bottom line is a short sale can save your credit from a devastating hit, but be prepared for some extra paperwork and time putting it together.

A Word of Caution

Run the numbers by your tax consultant before submitting a short-sale package to the lender. The IRS may deem forgiven funds a tax liability.

This chapter covered briefly how you can use a lease-option as a short-term solution when your house won't sell. Another option is keep your home as a long-term investment property. How to do that is covered in the next chapter.

CHAPTER 8

Renting and Keeping Your Home as an Investment

Traditionally, real estate is one of the more stable investments, with a track record of climbing values. True, local markets wax hot and cold as the market pendulum swings back and forth. But, with each swing the values stay a little higher and the lows never come back. This is because land is finite. There's only so much land, and it isn't expanding.

In Chapter 7 we discussed short-term lease-option strategies for creating cash flow when you can't sell a home. In that case, your goal is to get out of the house with as much equity as possible and time is not on your side. Renters are hard on homes, making them more difficult to sell—not a good thing in this case.

But there's another option where time *is* on your side, where the lemon becomes lemonade. And that option is to keep your starter home as a long-term investment or rental. This can be a good financial move for the following reasons:

1. Values of houses go up, especially over the long term. How often have you heard someone say they wished they had bought land or homes in a certain location before values skyrocketed?

2. There are tax deductions when you own it and tax breaks when you sell it. You—not a Wall Street money manager—control your investment.

3. You rent-proof the house and develop landlord skills to keep your investment in good condition.

147

4. Once you have developed some landlord skills you can buy other properties and accumulate a real-estate portfolio.

5. If you want to start a family business that is rewarding and profitable, this can be a good jumping-off point to buying and rehabing properties to keep or sell.

For example, Jerry and Carolyn lived in a typical blue-collar suburb. They built their first home, a modest two-bedroom brick bungalow, and lived in it for nine years. During those years they paid off their mortgage, and as their family grew they decided to build a bigger four-bedroom ranch with a full basement.

Fortunately, Jerry worked for a large mining company and had a good enough income that they could afford to build their new home without selling the old one. They rented out their first home, with the rents going into a special investment fund.

About a year later, a home up the block from their rental came on the market and they bought it, using their investment fund for a 20 percent down, nonowner-occupied mortgage. They rented this home out and used the rental income of both properties plus an additional $200 a month to pay off this mortgage in under six years.

These investors continued to buy and pay off properties over the years, and by the time Jerry retired they had seven homes, six of them mortgage free. Since renting and taking care of these properties was not their idea of retirement, they sold the homes and carried the financing themselves on 30-year mortgages. This meant that the income stream from the mortgages was mostly interest and created a huge boost to their retirement income.

Advantages and Disadvantages of Renting Your Home

You may not want to accumulate this many homes, but if you could keep your first starter home and let the tenants pay off the mortgage you would have a great investment. After twenty years the home should be nearly paid off and the value increased many times. However, as with any other investments, there are pros and cons. But first, here are the advantages.

Your Home Can Be a Good Rental Investment

Typical home buyers buy their first home with a low-money-down mortgage and move up to a larger home when kids come along or income goes up. They feel that to move up they need as big a down payment as possible, which entails selling their existing home.

But, there are alternative ways to go. Since mortgage qualifying is more credit driven than in the past, going with a large down payment is optional if you have good credit. That means it's now easier than ever before to keep your home for an investment.

To make this even easier, your mortgage lender will credit a good percentage of the home's rent as income to help you qualify for your next home. Indeed, the deck is stacked in your favor to become a real estate investor.

Some advantages of owning rental homes are:

■ Property taxes, mortgage interest, and landlord costs are just a few of the items you can deduct come April 15th. But first, get with your tax advisor and see the impact a rental will have on your tax situation.

■ You accumulate equity two ways:

1. As real estate values go up in the area, your investments go up too.

2. Rents pay off the mortgage. And rents usually go up, but the mortgage payment doesn't. That means you should be able to put more money in paying off your investment as time goes on.

■ This can be a great way to save money for kids' college, retirement or whatever. It also gives you a real estate asset you can borrow against and get the lowest interest home equity rates in case of an emergency.

■ If you move to another area, you can sell the home under a 1031 exchange and move your equity to another property and defer paying capital gains.

■ You can sometimes trade a single family up to a duplex or larger home if you find being a landlord is your calling. Investors occasionally find small apartments too much to handle and are willing to trade down. You can even exchange for building lots or raw land.

The Downsides of Turning Your Home into a Rental

Unfortunately, there's always a flip side, and with owning rentals it's no different. Before you venture very far down the landlord path, consider the following:

■ The average homeowner moves every few years and you may not have the time to build up equity.

■ Being a landlord is not for everyone. If you aren't the handy type and don't have an extra dose of patience, you may have a steep learning curve. If you're unsure about what's involved, talk to a few landlords and read a book or two about land-lording.

■ Real estate is usually a long-term investment. The longer you keep the property the better the return. Unless you're in a super-heated market you should expect that it will take five years or more to build a good level of equity.

■ If you need all the equity out of your present home to get into your next one, keeping the home for a rental may not be a sound financial move.

If you do decide that renting your home is something you can get excited about, the next section will give you an overview and some how-to suggestions to get started.

The Nuts and Bolts of Renting Your Home

The first key to being a successful landlord is treat your rental as the serious business it is. That means using good business practices, fol-lowing up promptly, and keeping your investment in good condition. This section will give you tips on how to do this. But first, you'll want to make a few changes to your home before you rent it out.

Defensive Decorating: Making Your Home Tenant Resistant

Few tenants take as good care of a home as the owners have done. And unfortunately, there's no good way to tell beforehand who are the good, the bad, or the destructive. So the best way is to make your home as damage proof as possible before you rent it out.

Figure 8-1 should give you some ideas on where to start. As you go along and gain experience, you'll see other areas you can change or improve.

Along with a little defensive decorating, inspecting the home every three months can head off potential problems. And catching problems early can save you bigger bucks later on and make landlording more fun.

FIGURE 8-1
Suggestions for making your home tenant resistant.

Item	Suggestions
Landscaping	Remove possible hazards to kids or pets. Install an auto-sprinkler system if you have grass that needs watering. Trim trees and shrubs that could damage the house.
Exterior	Make sure exterior is in good condition. Paint or re-side if needed. Tenants probably won't notify you until water damage is extensive.
Roof	Make sure roof is in good condition. If problems arise, you usually won't find out until it becomes a costly flood.
Kitchen and Bath Floor Coverings	Tile floors in bathrooms and kitchen are the best way to go. Running tile up the wall 4 inches or so in the bathrooms and kitchen is a good way to contain water that could destroy the sub-floor.
Floor Covering in Other Rooms	If you have wood floors, finish them with the most durable top-coating you can find. Replace carpeting and vinyl when it wears.
Plumbing and Fixtures	Do a walk-through inspection to check on all fixtures as often as possible. Leaks if not caught early will cause expensive problems.
Appliances	Check all appliances every three months. Make sure furnace filters are changed. In the West, swamp cooler water lines should be disconnected in the fall. Also, check the smoke-alarm batteries often. If tenants remove the 9-volt batteries to power other things, this can be a big liability item in case of a fire and the alarms not working.
Doors	Install cushioned door knob protectors on the walls where door knobs can dent the walls.
Walls	Installing chair rails and wainscoting are great ways to protect walls and make the home appealing.
Countertops	If you need to replace countertops, go with tile. It's tenant resistant and can be repaired more easily than other surfaces.

After you've got the home ready to rent, the next step is determine what you should charge.

How to Determine What to Charge for Rent

Determining what to rent your home for is similar to working up a sales price. You look at what comparable homes are renting for. Some sources for tracking down this information are:

- Call a couple of rental agencies in your area and see what they're renting similar homes to yours for.

- Check the "Homes for Rent" section in your local weekly or daily newspaper for similar rentals.

- If you know someone who is renting in the area, ask them what their rent is.

- If the rental market is hot in your area, consider starting out about 10 percent higher than what renters are currently paying. Their leases are probably several months old and don't reflect the current market. This can also hold true for a cool market, but you may have to come down if you don't get any bites.

The Art of Finding Good Tenants

Once you've decided on what rents to charge, it's important to set up a system to treat all callers equal by using the same criteria for evaluating potential tenants. You don't want to get into trouble over equal housing laws.

The first step is work up an application form or get one at a stationary store, along with rental or lease agreements. You can easily make up your own application form, but for the rental or lease form you should get a state- or city-approved form, or have your attorney put one together.

Questions you want to include on your application form are:

- Name, current address, and previous address if less than two years. Phone numbers—both home and cell phone.

- Employment: company, address, person to contact to verify job, phone numbers, how long on the job, and income. Job history is one of the most important items to zero in on. If they've been with a company for several years and have a stable employment history, they're likely to be a responsible tenant.

- Nearest relative, address, and phone.

- Current landlord, address, and phone. Also, it doesn't hurt to ask why they're moving.

- Credit references, such as credit cards, banks, credit unions, car loans, etc.

- The number of people that will be living in the house, including the number of children and pets.

It's important that you have every applicant fill out your form. Keep all applications dated and time stamped in a folder for a few months.

In the rare event you get challenged by an equal-housing checker posing as a renter, you have a paper trail proving you treated everyone equal and picked the successful applicant on merit.

Sometimes you'll get several applications in a morning after you've run an ad, and you're able to make a decision by that afternoon. The important thing is to tell your applicants when you'll get back to them and to make it as soon as possible. These people are looking at other rentals too and if you delay too long, you may lose them.

So how do you process these applications? First, spread them out and compare. As mentioned, job history is important; the number of children and pets is also a consideration. You may want to charge extra deposit for a pet. Ask around and find out what's normal for your area.

Credit is also a big criterion, assuming you have access to a credit reporting agency and they have signed a release on the application.

The next step is make your decision, then call the applicant and offer to rent them the house, and tell them how soon they'll need to get back to you with a deposit and first (or first and last) month's rent.

As a courtesy, call back the ones you didn't go with and tell them you've picked a tenant and thank them for considering your rental.

How to Handle the Cash Flow

You'll want to set up a separate checking account for your rental business. All deposits and rents should go through the account as well as the cost of any repairs and other expenses associated with the business. It's important to remember that the IRS is looking over your shoulder, so use good bookkeeping and accounting standards.

An important accounting item is the deposit. Make sure the rental agreement clearly shows the deposit amount and under what conditions it'll be returned or forfeited. If you have a lease-option clause, clearly differentiate how much is option money and how much is deposit.

In one case, the tenants moved out and wanted all their deposit back even though they had an option with a deadline. Because the paperwork didn't have a breakdown of the funds, the property owner had to return the total amount. The breakdown should have clearly spelled out $1,000 for a nonrefundable option and $100 for a deposit.

Finally, before the tenants move in, do a walk-through and list on the paperwork any damage such as dings in the walls, worn carpet or vinyl, dented appliances, and so on. Take photos or video to back up your list and have the tenants sign at the bottom of the list.

Give them the keys, and you're now a landlord: Let the fun begin.

Suggestions for Dealing with Tenants

There are many good books on the market that deal with landlording, and you may want to read a few to get an idea of how different landlords handle the job. Some basics to get you started are:

■ Prorate the rent so it falls on the first of the month. For example, if the rent is $1,000 a month and you rent the property on the 17th of July, that leaves 14 days to the first of August. Dividing $1,000 by 31 days equals $32.26 per day times the 14 days to cover the rent to August 1, or $451.61. On August 1, the tenant will then owe $1,451.61 for July and August, plus deposits. If it's customary in your area, do this with the last month's rent also.

The biggest reason you prorate the rent is to synchronize rent collections with the due date of your mortgage payment, which will likely be on the first of the month. Technically you probably have until the 15th to get the payment in before you incur a late charge, but this gives you a little wiggle room if the rent is late a day or two.

■ If you have the tenants mail you the rent, give them a stack of preaddressed envelopes. Some owners with more than one property use a different color envelope for each one.

■ Assess a late charge if the rent is late by five or more days. A surcharge of 4 or 5 percent of the rental amount is a good incentive for the tenant to get you the rent on time. Also, make sure your late fee is spelled out in the lease agreement.

■ If a prospective tenant can't come up with the first month and deposit up front, don't rent to them. Letting them pay the deposit over several months rarely works.

■ Never let tenants do work on your rental for credit unless they're professional tradesmen. It's tempting, but it seldom works out. You end up paying top dollar for bad painting, landscaping, or whatever.

■ Do an inspection walk-through as often as possible without harassing the tenants. Explain to them up front that you'll do a quick inspection every so often to make sure any problems are spotted early. You don't want small problems becoming major ones.

This happened to one landlord when he didn't inspect his rental. A water leak in the ceiling caused the Sheetrock to become saturated and crash down onto the kitchen floor one weekend. When he got word of the problem and went over on Monday morning, the tenants had already moved out. It was a huge mess and expense that could have been avoided by a quick inspection.

Tenants are not always vigilant in spotting or telling you promptly about a suspected problem.

Every landlord can add to this list, and as you gain experience you will too. If you find you like being a landlord, start thinking of adding another rental to your portfolio, perhaps even a home that can be converted into a duplex. But first, before you think about becoming a landlord, you'll need to know about zoning.

How Zoning and Covenant Restrictions Affect Rentals

Zoning and covenants have a big impact on landlords and knowing these restrictions are especially important if you turn your home into a rental.

For instance:

■ Many zoning laws restrict how many people can live in a house. If you have been thinking about buying a college town rental, you'll want to be aware of these limits. So, should your tenants decide to let a few relatives or friends live with them in violation of your lease, you'll need to take fast action.

Zoning laws enforce governmental restrictions, such as federal wetlands preservation and county and city zoning master plans. It is usually city zoning that determines whether you can turn that old house into a duplex.

■ CC&Rs (covenants, conditions, and restrictions) basically cover what you can and can't do with your home. CC&Rs are created when a subdivision is recorded. In addition, condos, co-ops, PUDs (planned unit developments), and any subdivision governed by a homeowners association and their elected directors can add restrictions.

If you don't pay your dues and follow the rules, they can take your hut and kick you off the island.

What Do CC&Rs Cover?

When developers create a subdivision, they survey the land parcel and draw up a map or plat that contains survey, engineering data, and other information. Next, they determine the amenities they'll include and what price they'll sell the lots for.

The developers want to sell their lots, so they work up some rules that buyers have to abide by if they want to build in that development. These rules or CC&Rs govern how big the houses can be, what they're constructed with, landscaping, and other restrictions.

In other words, the purpose of the CC&Rs is to protect the homeowner's investment because a home's value is largely dependent on the other homes around it. Obviously, expensive homes built among trailer parks is not a good mix.

Some developers put thought and planning into their covenants to project exclusivity and maximize the value of their project, while others are less serious and use mostly boilerplate wording.

So how does this affect you, as a seller or if you decide to keep your home as a rental?

1. Before you put your home up for sale, read the CC&Rs for any restrictions on *For Sale* signs. Some subdivisons and condo developments restrict or prohibit signs and brochure boxes.

2. In some developments, changes in colors, architectural design and structure, and landscaping are permissible only with the approval of the homeowners association.

3. If you have a home in an older area and want to remodel it into a duplex, you would first need to check zoning and any CC&Rs.

4. Before you rent your home, you should check CC&Rs for any restrictions.

CC&Rs in Action

Before you remodel your home or turn it into a rental, get a copy of the CC&R from the recorder's office or title company and read it carefully. A conflict with the homeowners association or ending up on the docket of the local magistrate can be expensive and isn't the best way to build neighbor goodwill.

In one example, Ron, who lived in an upscale subdivision, left for work early one day, when he noticed a crew tearing the roof off the Westons' home across the street. A routine roof replacement, he thought. But coming home from work that afternoon, he was astounded to find the roof gone and framing underway for a second story that would block his view of the Salt Lake City skyline.

Upset, Ron scanned the restrictive covenants attached to the back of his title policy. Section B clearly stated that no dwelling could be over 1 story if it would block a neighbor's view. He called the homeowners association president and pointed out the clear violation of the restrictions and demanded immediate action. The association president agreed and promised to talk with the homeowner immediately.

Mr. Weston was belligerent when confronted by the association president about the addition. He pointed out he had a valid building permit and didn't like neighbors telling him what he could do with his home, and he refused to stop construction.

The homeowners association attorney then got a restraining order stopping all work based on violation of the subdivision's restrictive covenants. Eventually, the Westons were forced to spend about $35,000 tearing down the framing and replacing the roof. Lesson learned the hard way: Read first and take your subdivision's covenants seriously before undertaking any changes or additions to your home.

What Are Some of the Most Common Restrictions?

Approval of architectural design, materials, dwelling cost, square footage, and landscaping are usually the higher profile restrictions. Others are setback and material requirements on garages, fences, storage sheds, and parking for trailered boats and RVs.

Restrictions can also attempt to maintain the historical nature of an area by requiring approval of paint colors, materials, or any improvements that deviate from the period norm. Also commonly covered are farm animals, storage and disposal of trash, soil and mining operations, drainage control, and trailers on the property.

Any CC&R provisions that violate local, state, or federal laws are void. A good example of a common restriction that was voided by legislative change is the clause barring minorities from buying property in many areas, which some developers had written into CC&Rs fifty or so years ago. Also, the Americans with Disabilities Act of 1990 has mandated changes when some older rentals are upgraded.

Zoning Restrictions

Zoning and land use restrictions are different from CC&Rs. These are governmental restrictions that govern what you can do with your plot of land. They range from federal wetland restrictions to city zoning.

Your first move should be a call to your town's zoning department. In most towns, subdivisions zoning laws limit houses to single-family occupancy. If the tenant is a relative you shouldn't have a problem with adding an in-law apartment. Most zoning departments, insurers, and mortgage lenders will go along with that kind of addition.

But if you want to create an apartment and rent to a nonrelative, check the zoning first. If prohibited you may be able to get a conditional-use permit or variance. This entails going to the zoning department and filling out the paperwork. There may be restrictions on how utilities are set up as well as inspections for building code compliance. A hearing may also be required to give the neighbors a chance to protest.

True, this is a more expensive and time-consuming way to go, but in the end it'll be worth it. Some homeowners ignore zoning rules because the city or county is lax in enforcement and they know they can get away with it. They possibly can for a while, but it usually comes back to haunt them. Administrations change and all properties eventually are put up for sale. If they sell or refinance, a mortgage lender may want to see the permits. Or the insurance company may deny a claim if you've violated the policy terms and your home is a pile of ashes.

Ignoring Zoning and Permits Can Come Back to Haunt You

Keith and Holly found this out the hard way when they had to sell a home they converted several years ago into a duplex by finishing the full basement.

The apartment had been rented out for years. Several other homes on the street also had basement apartments, no one had questioned the zoning, and the city had never complained.

When the sellers put up the sale sign, they quickly found a buyer who made an acceptable offer. The paperwork went to a mortgage lender who ordered an appraisal. However, when the appraiser checked the zoning she found it was zoned single family, and she adjusted her appraisal downward.

The sellers were upset and called the city zoning department. Zoning officials said although they hadn't and wouldn't enforce the zoning in the area, they still wouldn't approve a change to duplex zoning.

This created a sticky situation. As a single-family house the house was appraised at $16,000 under the sales price, and now the genie was out of the bottle: The home couldn't be sold as a duplex. Furthermore, no mortgage lender would finance an illegal duplex.

The buyers, rather than walking away from the deal, offered to buy at the reduced price. Reluctantly the sellers accepted; they didn't have much choice at this point.

Did the buyers get a great deal? They bought a home with a basement apartment they could rent out (still technically illegally) and cover a big part of the mortgage payment. But there were strings still attached: It was only a good deal as long as they lived there. If they wanted to sell, the home could still go for only a single-family house. But with the rent from the basement apartment, they could build some fast equity.

Another possibility is get city hall to change the street to duplex zoning. Time is on the owner's side, because areas change and city administrations change.

In another situation, an enterprising carpenter bought an older home in a good area and completely gutted it. He rebuilt the home complete with gingerbread trim and period color scheme. When he put it on the market a few years later, a full-price offer came in hours after the sign went up. About two weeks into the sale, a condition came back from the mortgage company doing the buyer's loan. The lender wanted copies of the building permit and any paperwork verifying the home had passed the inspections during the rebuilding. Luckily, the seller had kept the paperwork and was able to satisfy the lender's request.

The bottom line is that before you rebuild, or convert an attic or basement into an apartment, get the proper permits and verify zoning (and keep the paperwork). It may cost you some fees or increase your property taxes, but by not complying you can get nailed big time when you sell.

Selling Your Home After It Has Been a Rental

If you decide to sell your home after it's been a rental, there are a few restrictions you'll want to know about. First, usually you can sell your home as a primary residence if you live in it for two of the last five years. This basically allows you to rent your home for up to three years before selling it.

Interestingly, this rule is tailor-made for those who have a hard time selling and have to do a rent/option or wait for the market to change. Before selling, check with your tax advisor to see how the numbers impact your situation.

Second, if you're moving or want to defer capital gains taxes, consider going with a 1031 tax-free exchange.

The 1031 Tax-Deferred Exchange

This underutilized financial tool can make a big difference in the following situations:

1. You want to keep your starter home for a rental when you move up.

2. You've rented part of your home and it's subject to capital gains.

3. You want to trade your single family up to a duplex or fourplex.

4. Someone has an investment property (single-family rental, duplex, or even new construction) you would like, but if they sold, capital gains would kick in.

The possibilities are endless for creating win-win deals and deferring capital gains to a time when the tax bite is not so painful.

Unfortunately, paying capital gains taxes keeps many owners from selling single-family homes and condos they've owned for years and would like to unload. These properties may be homes they couldn't sell in a slow market, and so they rented them. Eventually, the market changed and suddenly the rental has lots of equity and a growing tax liability.

Not wanting to go through the pain of fixing up the property and putting it on the market, many owners continue living with the problem and procrastinating doing something proactive. As equity grows, the problem grows for many owners.

Luckily, a 1031 exchange may be able to solve their problem by getting them into something more suited to their interests.

Putting a 1031 exchange together is fairly straightforward but may require the expertise of an exchange intermediary, accountant, and a title/escrow company, depending on the number and complexity of the properties. The exchange intermediary is the neutral party that handles the nuts and bolts of the exchange. To find one, look in the yellow pages or check the Internet under Real Estate Exchange. Or better still, Realtors and title companies who do 1031 exchanges will be able to recommend good intermediaries. You'll also need a title or escrow company to handle title work and funding. And, of course, you'll need the purchase contracts of those who are buying and selling the properties involved in the exchange.

The exciting thing about 1031 exchanges is you don't have to have two property owners who want to exchange straight across, you can bring in other buyers and sellers with their properties to add to the mix.

Here's a simplified example. You find a buyer for the property you want to get rid of (relinquished property) and the sale goes into escrow. You have 45 days to find a property you want to buy (replacement property) and that goes into escrow. The buy/sell mix closes and you end up with the property you want. The party with the least equity can use cash or financing to make up the difference.

How One Couple Profited from a 1031 Exchange

When Norm and Sandy were transferred from Utah to Georgia the market was slow. They couldn't sell the home they were living in nor a smaller rental home they bought from an estate. So, they hired a rental company to manage the homes, both of which rented for close to their mortgage payments.

Three years later, when interest rates had dropped and the market had improved, Norm and Sandy decided to sell the homes. Their strategy was to put the proceeds from the sales into a 1031 exchange escrow with a title company in Utah and find a rental property in Georgia. When they closed on the property where they lived, the funds would be released from escrow and used for a down payment. The balance of the purchase price would come from a nonowner-occupied mortgage.

Luckily, the tenants in the smaller home wanted to buy it and were able to qualify for the mortgage payments, which were $80 less than their rent payment. The sale closed and the $37,000 proceeds went into the title company exchange department's escrow account.

While the paperwork for the rental sale was going forward, Norm and Sandy were out looking for rentals in their area. The market was tight and they didn't find anything they liked until two weeks after their home in Utah had closed. (The IRS allows 45 days to identify a property and up to 180 days to close the deal.) They made an offer on a two-bedroom condo in a good area for $185,000, and it was accepted.

The $37,000 in escrow was used for a 20 percent down payment and the balance financed with a nonowner-occupied mortgage. The equity from one rental home in Utah was transferred to Georgia with no capital gains taxes.

Norm and Sandy's other rental has six months to go on a lease. If the tenants can't or don't want to buy it, it'll go on the market and the process will be repeated.

As you can see, the 1031 exchange is a great way to transfer equity from one area to another and deferring capital gains taxes. If you're in a difficult market, and you need to move and can't sell your home, you can rent it until the market improves and still build equity.

Rules for a 1031 Exchange

The IRS requires the exchange to be like-in-kind, and it identifies that as real estate for real estate. You can exchange a duplex for bare land, office building, warehouse, or whatever. Just so it's real estate.

You can exchange one property for ten properties—the numbers on either side of the exchange don't matter.

From the date of closing on the sale of the relinquished property, you have 45 days to find the replacement property(s), and 180 days to close.

You must insert a clause into all sale contracts that identify the transactions as a 1031 exchange. The IRS needs to see an easy-to-follow paper trail.

John and Angie went the exchange route when they decided they no longer wanted the demands of being a landlord. They owned a duplex that had about $80,000 in equity, and they didn't want to pay out a big part of their equity in taxes. Although they didn't want to exchange for more rental property, undeveloped land appeared to be a good way to go: low maintenance, no rent to collect, and no late night plumbing problems to fix.

Finding a buyer for their duplex was easy and the sale closed with the proceeds going into escrow. Their Realtor found a ten-acre parcel for sale that appeared to be in the path of eventual development.

Since the land cost $139,000, John and Angie needed about $59,000 to make a deal. They decided to take out a ten-year, low-interest equity line of credit on their home for the funds needed to complete the deal. The second leg of the 1031 exchange closed and everyone was happy.

As a result of the exchange, a young couple starting out was able to buy a duplex they had been searching for. John and Angie won't have to collect rents or do maintenance on their days off. Everyone wins and the taxman has to wait for another day to collect his due.

Figure 8-2 is a list of the typical steps involved in a 1031 tax-deferred exchange. For more information on 1031 exchanges, go to *www.firstamex.com*

Renting Co-Ops and Condos

Renting co-ops and condos presents some challenges that renting single-family homes don't have, namely:

- Few owners remain active in the homeowners association when they move out and rent their unit. This is unfortunate because the association can enact rules, defer maintenance, or develop management problems that can directly affect your investment.

- In your lease or rental agreement you may want to add an escalator clause that the rent can go up if the homeowners association dues increase.

- Your condo or co-op may have restrictions on renting the unit. Co-ops especially may not allow you to rent to anyone without the board's approval.

- If the units in the project reach 50 percent rentals, you may have trouble selling. Mortgage lenders are reluctant to make loans in high rental projects.

- You'll want to take extra care picking tenants. If you rent to people who like to party or who are not inclined to follow the rules, it can cost you. Fines and assessments go against the unit (owner), not the tenants.

- Make sure your tenants carry a renter's insurance policy. For example, if there is a water leak that affects the units below, you could have a liability problem.

FIGURE 8-2
Typical steps in a 1031 tax-deferred exchange.

Steps	What's Involved
The property for sale is listed and a property exchange intermediary is lined up. The intermediary can be a title company or an attorney who is experienced in exchanges.	Include a notice in the listing and sales documents that the property is part of a 1031 exchange. As a seller you will assign the role of grantee or transferee of the deed to the intermediary.
Buyer for property is found.	The intermediary prepares an assignment assigning the role of seller to the intermediary along with the other exchange paperwork, which goes to the closing agent.
The sale is closed and equity funds are put into escrow.	The exchanger and the buyer sign an assignment agreement, which assigns the intermediary the role of seller in the sale. The 45-day clock starts ticking on identifying an exchange property.
The hunt for a replacement property should be well on its way by this time.	There are 45 days to find property and identify it in writing by street address or legal description. This information is faxed to the intermediary.
Exchanger makes offer on property.	Included in the purchase agreement is a notice that the deal is part of a 1031 exchange with the required assignments. This usually is not a problem with the sellers; they just want their money and be on their way.
What if there are multiple properties and multiple exchangers?	All the legs of the exchange are put into escrow and closed with each party getting its designated property at about the same time. Closing and funding has to be within the 180 days.
Tax forms are filed.	Exchangers file Form 8824 with the IRS and file any other state-required forms.

How to Build a Real Estate Portfolio

Renting your home can be a great way to get started in building a real estate portfolio.

You undoubtedly financed your first home with a low down-payment loan since it was owner occupied. You can probably buy your next home with a low down payment as well. If you're willing to move every few years you can accumulate several rental properties with favorable mortgages by living in them for a couple of years.

After you start accumulating equity and a track record, you can finance with a nonowner-occupied mortgage. Normally, these loans require at least 20 percent down. But, with good credit and a growing net worth, there are nonowner-occupied loans available with 10 percent down or less.

For most people, selling their home means buying another at the same time or shortly thereafter. The next chapter shows you how to switch hats and get the best deal as a buyer.

CHAPTER 9

Buying Your Next Home

Many home sellers who sell their home have purchased another or plan to do so in the near future. It may be a move up, a move down, or a hope that they can equal what they had before moving. But one thing is certain, the sale of one home is closely tied to buying another.

Even though you've been through the buying process before, real estate changes fast and continually, especially in the mortgage arena. So, you may want to consider this chapter a refresher course that can save you a lot of money and frustration.

Remember when a buyer made an offer on your home and how concerned you were that they could afford it? And when the buyers produced a letter from their lender verifying they were good to go, how you had that bird-in-the-hand feeling?

Well, now you get to put on a buyer's hat and tread the path to giving sellers a warm, fuzzy feeling so they will accept your offer. But first a look at what credit scores you'll need to get the best loan.

It's All About the Credit Score

If it's been a few years since you bought your last home, you'll find mortgage qualifying has changed. It's now more about your credit score: a three-digit number that's generated from the data in your credit report.

The best terms go to those who have credit scores 700 or higher. And you get high credit scores by paying bills on time, keeping account balances low, and not maxing out credit cards and accounts.

How the Numbers Affect Your Payments

As an example of how important credit scores are, suppose your credit report came back with a 620 score. That's only 80 points under 700, but those points could cost you thousands of dollars.

The table below illustrates how your credit score can change your interest rate and your monthly payments on a 30-year, $100,000 loan. As you can see, trashing your credit could cost you an extra $270 a month (the difference between the highest and lowest FICO score).

FICO Score	Interest Rate	Monthly Principal/Interest Payment
720–850	5.300%	$555.30
700–719	5.425%	$563.09
675–699	5.963%	$597.17
620–674	7.113%	$672.91
560–619	8.531%	$771.11
500–559	9.289%	$825.50

The message here is clear. If you're planning on selling your home and buying another, look at your credit score and take corrective action before putting your home on the market.

Credit Improvement Kit

Normally, improving your overall credit score can take a year or more. But, if you need a few points to clear the bar, here are some suggestions:

- Obviously, the first step is pull up your credit report and see where you're at. You can get one through the Internet at *www .myfico.com* if you don't have a mortgage lender yet.

- Look for errors, such as accounts that aren't yours, late payments that were made on time, debts paid off but show as outstanding, or old debts that should be removed. Negatives should be deleted after seven years, but bankruptcies can stay on for ten years.

- Pay down balances on credit cards and other accounts as much as possible.

- Don't go over 30 days past due on any payments.

- Forget about grace periods and make payments before they're due.

- Keep your balance as low as you can.

- Don't close out unused or zero balance accounts. This can hurt you by changing the total debt to available credit ratio. If this ratio is high, it'll appear you're maxing your accounts, which can cost you points.

- If you do cut up credit cards or close accounts, keep the oldest one open. How long you've had credit is another consideration.

Once you've got a good idea of what your credit situation is, the next step is find a good mortgage lender. Don't assume the mortgage company you have your present loan with has the best rates or cheapest costs—try surfing the Net for mortgage deals.

Finding a Lender on the Internet

Surfing the Net is a great way to get a feel for loan options and rates, and you can even get a good loan over the Net. However, the biggest caveat to watch out for is teaser rates. As mentioned before, a teaser rate is lower than the current market rate. The lender will try to make up the loss with padded fees or not be able to deliver when it's time to lock in the advertised interest rate.

For instance, if the financial markets are quoting mortgage rates at 6.0 percent that day and a Web lender hits you with 5.90 percent to get you to respond to their ad, you've encountered a teaser rate. You can be sure the mortgage company isn't going to lose money, so they'll make it up in the closing costs or discount points.

If in your surfing you find a Web lender that's a national bank or mortgage company, they may refer you to a loan officer at one of their branch offices closest to you. Other lenders may handle everything by mail, phone, and e-mail, with the closing handled by a local title company. Either way can work out.

Credit Information Sites on the Web Worth Checking Out Are:

www.myfico.com is the Web site of Fair Isaac Corp. that created the popular FICO score. You can also click on "products," and for a fee you get three major credit reports plus the use of their simulator. This allows you to see how paying off a loan or lowering a certain credit card balance could affect your credit score and in turn the amount of loan you can qualify for.

www.bankrite.com has a FICO score estimator and other good credit information.

How to Compare Loans on the Web

Most mortgage Web sites have prequalifying worksheets, where you can fill in your debts, income, and maximum house price and get instant ratios and other loan data.

If you want to go further, the next step is preapproval. You fill out a more detailed questionnaire, provide a credit card number for a credit report, and hit "submit." Within a few hours you'll be contacted by phone or e-mail.

Some Good Web-Lender Sites to Check Out Are:

www.countrywide.com

www.e-loan.com

www.getsmart.com

www.loanweb.com

www.quickenloans
.quicken.com

www.wellsfargo.com

The first step in using an e-loan site, for example, is a prequalification questionnaire. You enter data about your income, debts, and down payment. The site calculates your ratios and tells you if your numbers look good. To continue, you can click on "apply" and fill out more detailed data along with your social security number.

Most sites have loan comparison charts that let you look at the numbers side by side. On e-loan, one interesting column lists various interest rates you can get by paying up to 3 points. Each point, as we previously covered, equals 1 percent of the loan amount. If you happen to see a loan option you like, click on "apply" to go to the prequalification site, and the site will guide you through the process.

After you've decided on which lender you want to go with, have her give you a prequalification letter verifying you're good to go.

If you're a little rusty on how to shop for the best areas, identify your dream house, and present offers, check out my previous book on buying a home, *A Survival Guide for Buying a Home* (New York: AMACOM, 2004), for more specifics.

In the happy event you've got a sale pending on your present home, you'll need to take a few precautions if you find another home you want to write an offer on.

You've Sold Your Home and Found Another One

With all your ducks lined up in a row, it's shopping time. But before you hit the road looking at homes and making an offer, there are a couple of items you need to be aware of.

First, if your home hasn't closed yet, you'll need to make any offers contingent upon your home closing. Ideally, the closing on your new home should be on the same day as your old one, or as close thereafter as possible.

Second, coordinate the moving schedule so you can move from your old home right into the new one. This may sound paranoid, but if you move out of your old home and for some reason the sale falls through, it can get ugly—the kind of migraine over-the-counter pain killers won't touch.

Yes, it happens, sales do fall through at the last minute. Buyers get into accidents, get sick, disappear, have heart attacks, go to jail, get divorced, get cold feet, and so on to infinity. So stay flexible and plan for the worst, but hope for the best as you write up an offer on your next dream home. With that in mind, it's time to look at homes.

Develop Your Dream House Shopping List

Since you've owned one or more homes, you've likely developed some ideas of what you want in your next home. To help you transfer those ideas onto paper you may want to fill out the following two worksheets.

First, get everyone together who will live in the new house and make a list of six or more things you love about your *present* home and location and things you don't like. This will help you decide what features you'll need to create the lifestyle you want.

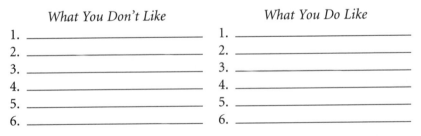

What You Don't Like	*What You Do Like*
1. _____	1. _____
2. _____	2. _____
3. _____	3. _____
4. _____	4. _____
5. _____	5. _____
6. _____	6. _____

Once you've listed what you like and don't like in homes and areas, the next step is listing your needs and wants.

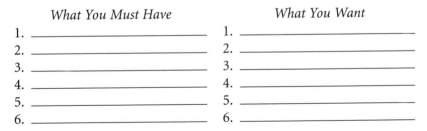

What You Must Have	*What You Want*
1. _____	1. _____
2. _____	2. _____
3. _____	3. _____
4. _____	4. _____
5. _____	5. _____
6. _____	6. _____

It's also important to ask yourself what kind of house will make a home. For example, if you have children, a family room next to the kitchen or a more open floor plan may be better than the formal floor plan found in many colonials. Crystallizing your thinking and making lists before you look will save a lot of time and frustration.

Working Up a Wants and Needs List

Start by asking yourself the following questions:

1. Do you want to move closer to work than your present home and cut down on commuting time? How far are you willing to drive or how much time are you willing to spend commuting? The answers will determine the radius of your search area.

2. How far away are the schools and is busing required? If you're interested in a certain school, verify the boundaries with the school district because they can change yearly.

3. Do you like your present home style? Do you want to change and why?

4. What type of floor plan will be the most compatible with your lifestyle?

5. How close do you need to be to shopping, churches, medical and recreational facilities?

Narrowing Down Your Choices

Go over the list you've worked up carefully with your agent so she can enter your preferences in the MLS computer. Matching your criteria against the thousands of homes on the market will take only a few minutes. The resulting printout should contain only those homes in your price range and locations, with the amenities you selected.

How many homes do you need to look at? On the average most buyers who know what they want narrow the list down to between five and twelve homes. Still, it's possible the first, second, or third home you see could be love at first sight. In that case, it's a good idea to accelerate the search and eliminate the rest of the homes on your list. Also have your agent update the list for any similar homes to the one you like that may have just come on the market. If the computer comes up with no comparable homes then you'll probably want to write an offer right away! Time is of the essence here, especially if you're sitting on an offer on your home and the time-to-closing clock is ticking.

But suppose you can't find the home you want and you've got 30 days until your present home closes. What do you do then?

Ryan and Sue had this problem when they sold their home. They wanted to move into a neighborhood so their three kids could attend a certain school district, but none of the houses they liked were on the market.

Being resourceful under pressure, Sue put together a flier with a picture of her family and a short letter outlining why they wanted to live in the area, asking anyone who was thinking of selling to call them.

A week after passing out about seventy-five fliers, Ryan and Sue got a call from a couple about to retire, who had been thinking of downsizing and moving to a warmer state. The flier prompted the couple to decide that opportunity is knocking and that now was the time to move.

Upon inspecting the home, Ryan and Sue found it was just what they had been looking for, and they made an offer. They were hoping for a quick closing since the closing on their present home was in three weeks. It didn't work out quite like they wanted. The owners couldn't move out in three weeks but needed a 60-day closing.

To make the deal work, Ryan and Sue rented a storage unit and stayed with his parents for about a month until they could close.

It's amazing how often potential sellers are galvanized into action when they hear a qualified buyer ready to buy is interested in the area.

If you can't find the existing home you want—and many move-up home buyers can't—you may consider another option, which is building a new home. From living in your old home, you've probably developed some neat ideas you would like to try. Okay, that's great, but to make those neat ideas happen you'll need to work with a builder. That presents a new set of challenges that we cover in the next section.

Buying New Construction

Like buying a new car, there's something about the smells, fresh paint, and newly installed carpet in a new house. Many move-up home buyers feel this is the way to go; they don't want to redo someone else's decorating and landscaping again. If this is the route you want to go, this section will show you how to avoid the pitfalls many people make selling their home and buying new construction.

Don't Make These Expensive Mistakes

Many sellers who buy new homes and have a house to sell first feel they have two to three months to sell their old home, so what's the hurry. They wait as long as possible to put their home on the market hoping they won't have to move twice. Here's why you don't want to do that:

1. If your timing is off, you could lose a sizable deposit. Builders have a narrow time window to close when the home is done. The construction loan interest clock doesn't stop until the permanent loan closes.

2. It's better to put your home on the market immediately and, if it sells fast, have an apartment or family you can bunk with for a month or two. The big advantages are that your home is sold and your equity is safely in the bank.

3. Sales can and do fail for many reasons, and experienced agents can give you dozens of war stories of sales failing at the last minute for bizarre and off-the-wall reasons. You want to avoid having a sale fail and not having time to find another buyer before the closing deadline. A done deal is when the check is in the bank.

4. Granted, in a hot market, where homes sell in short order, the above advice may seem a little paranoid, but even in these markets it's best to give yourself a margin. A good way to do this is have a backup offer waiting in the wings. In hot markets, this is usually easy to do because there are more buyers for fewer houses, and backup offers become the norm.

5. If your home doesn't sell or the sale fails, see if your builder will take your home on trade. That is, the builder buys your home— plan on a 10 to 15 percent discount—so you can buy the new home. In one subdivision, the builder had a lucrative side business selling the homes he took in on trade.

With that out of the way, the next section looks at how to find that new home.

Shopping the Developments

The first step after you've got that loan commitment in hand is make a list of the new communities in the area you're interested in. Before you waste a lot of time driving around, call and find out the median price of the homes. Don't go by the starting price in the advertising. Projects rarely have homes or even sell homes at the bottom of the advertised price range.

From the builder's standpoint, the name of the game is to upgrade you to the maximum you can qualify for. Before that can happen they have to get out to the models.

It's similar to buying a car. You may be attracted by the low advertised price and when you get there you find it's a stripped down model. The salesperson then pressures you to upgrade. New-home builders are masters of this. By the time you get through the options and upgrades, the real price range starts about halfway up the scale. If you plan on this from the beginning you'll save a lot of running around. This is not to say that builders are dishonest, just that new home marketing stretches the envelope a little to get people through their projects.

Ten New Home-Buyer Tips

1. Builders often try to pressure you to use their lender. They want to minimize deals falling through, and controlling the financing is one way to do this. They may offer you upgrades or buydowns to go with their financing. Of course, the best way to find out whether these incentives are really free is to get a good faith estimate from the builder's lender. Compare it with estimates from a couple of other lenders and the best deal will become obvious. You'll often find that the teaser interest rates advertised will cost you and that you can get just as good or a better deal with another lender.

If you do find a better deal than the builder is offering, get a qualifying letter from your lender. This should satisfy most builders that you're a genuine, qualified buyer.

Homebuilder Web Sites

www.homebuilder.com

www.newhomesdirect.com

www.newhomesale.com

www.homegain.com.

2. Get copies of the CC&R (Covenants, Conditions, & Restrictions) and HOA (homeowners association) rules. Read them over carefully because these documents will tell you what you can and can't do with your home. For example, you might be prohibited from parking RVs next to your home or be restricted in what landscaping you can do.

One home buyer had a motor home that he wanted to keep on an extended driveway next to his home. Unfortunately, he didn't read the CC&Rs before he bought. When he started to work on his driveway extension, he found out quickly that RVs were not allowed on the home sites. This ended up costing him $35 a month at an RV storage facility about a mile away.

3. Research the builder. Check with the Better Business Bureau and a state contractor's board if you have one. Research not only the company but the builder's name. You want to know whether there have been complaints filed, if so how many, and whether the builder has gone bankrupt recently. If the company or builder has lots of complaints, seriously consider shopping elsewhere.

4. Walk around the community and talk to at least three new homeowners. Ask them how they like the builder and how fast problems or complaints are handled. Especially important, find out how many items were on their punch list and how long it took the builder to take care of them. The *punch list* is a list of mistakes, problems, or anything the builder has to take care of that you find during your final walk-through. If the new owners tell you the punch list is more than a dozen items and repair is slow, that's a red flag.

5. Ask the sales person or builder's rep how close to the completion date homes are finished. If possible, get a copy of the construction schedule. If the builder is behind a month or two on projections, this may cause you problems if you have to be out of a home or rental on a certain date. This is another red flag.

6. If you find a model you absolutely love and want to put a deal together, make sure you get everything you want in writing. An often used saying in real estate, painfully learned and relearned, is: "If it isn't in writing it doesn't exist." Verbal promises are nothing more than hot air because you can't enforce anything not in writing.

7. Get a price list of the options and upgrades. Don't ever sign any paperwork unless you know exactly what an item costs. "To be filled in later" is an absolute no-no. Also, never leave the sales office without copies of all the paperwork. Too many buyers run into problems later because they didn't get copies of addendums covering upgrades and options.

Nathan and Laurie had this happen when they bought a home in the first phase of a new community. The salesman told them a fireplace—a $2,500 option—was included in the model they picked out, and they took his word for it. Several weeks later when they did a framing walk-through, they noticed the concrete and framing for a fireplace was missing.

As it turned out a fireplace for that model was not standard, and the salesperson who had written up the sales contract no longer worked for the builder. You guessed it, there was nothing in the paperwork about a fireplace. Nathan and Laurie had to write a check for half the option or $1,250 to get it added, with the balance due in thirty days. Obviously, they weren't too happy about it, but there was nothing they could do without losing a sizable deposit if they backed out.

8. It can't be stressed too strongly that you need to make sure you get copies of all documents and number the addendums 1/x, 2/x, etc. Missing addendums usually cause the most problems because that's where changes and contract modifications are written.

9. Make sure you understand the paragraphs in the purchase contract about when you close. Builders often pressure you to close before the house is finished or before the punch items are completed. You don't want to close before all items are done, so deal with this up front and get it in writing on an addendum if you have to.

10. Before you buy a new home, consider reading a highly recommended book, *The Ultimate New-Home Buying Guide*, by Jeff and Susan Treganowan.

A Final Caution if Your Home Hasn't Closed Yet

When writing up an offer and your home hasn't sold or closed yet, you'll want to include the clauses listed below. Depending on your state's paperwork, you either write in or check the appropriate boxes to protect you in case something unforeseen should happen:

Web Sites for Checking Out Neighborhoods

www.realtor.com

www.homeadvisor.com

www.homeSeekers.com

www.cyberhomes.com

www.iOwn.com

www.realestatebook.com

www.revillage.com

www.Owners.com

www.homesdatabase.com

www.homeroute.com.

■ As mentioned previously, make your offer subject to your home closing if you have an offer pending. If your home isn't sold, you'll make it subject to finding a buyer within a specified time period.

■ Make the offer subject to professional home inspection. If the inspector finds problems you have a way out.

■ Coordinate your closing and moving dates with your buyers and the sellers of the home you're buying. You don't want everyone trying to move into and out of the houses at the same time.

■ Make your offer subject to a final loan approval as a precaution.

If everything meshes the way it should, you'll get the fun and exciting job of moving into a new home. But before closing, there's a lot of work to do, including garage sales—the more you get rid of the less you have to move—and rounding up a mover. Tips on how to do this are the focus of the next chapter.

CHAPTER **10**

Decluttering, Moving, and Yard Sales

Although we have emphasized this point throughout the book, it's so important that it bears repeating: The key to selling fast and getting the best offer is to appeal to a buyer's emotions.

Buyers looking for their dream home usually make offers on homes only if they can envision themselves living there. That means imagining their couch in the living or family room, their big screen HDTV in a family room corner, their pictures on the walls, their table in the kitchen, and their king-size water bed in the master bedroom. One of the cheapest and fastest ways to make this happen is to declutter. In other words, you remove anything not essential to daily living and put it in outside storage, a corner of the basement, or in the garage.

True, "not essential to daily living" can mean different things to different homeowners. However, Realtors have found through experience that there are some common items that can cost you big bucks or slow down the sale; we'll cover those in detail in this chapter.

Also, since you're going to be moving stuff, this chapter will show you not only what to move, but how to find a good mover, and how to hold money-making garage sales. But first, the fun part, decluttering.

Decluttering Can Make You Money

If buyers lose focus because they're distracted by your stuff, it's likely they'll lose interest in your house and move on to the next home on

179

their list. When this happens several times in a row, it's a strong clue that something is wrong.

Donna had this problem when she and Ted, her husband, became empty nesters and decided to buy a smaller home. The big problem was an overflowing twenty-year collection of dolls, doll clothes, and accessories. In two unused bedrooms, boxes were piled to the ceiling. The family room had three glass display cases of dolls and accessories. Even the living room had a display case of antique dolls. The owners had tried to sell the home on their own for about sixty days without any action. They had lots of people come to the house, but they would do a quick walk-through and mumble a polite "thank you" as they left.

Feeling discouraged, they decided to see what a Realtor could do to get things moving. A friend recommended an agent they had used with good success, so Donna called and asked him to come out and see what it would take to sell their home.

The agent walked through the home and made some notes on a clipboard. After completing the tour he sat down at the kitchen table with the sellers. In short, he told them their "stuff" would have to go and suggested they rent a storage unit and move out all the boxes, display cases, and everything else not needed. He gave them a list he worked up of what needed to go into storage, and made an appointment to come back in a few days.

Donna and Ted were not too happy about moving what seemed like everything in the house into storage. But they knew it was probably the only way they would get their home sold.

With the help of many family members and a couple of friends with pickups, they spent the weekend moving out everything on the list the agent had given them. They didn't realize they had accumulated so much stuff in the last twenty years.

The result was dramatic: Removing all the extra stuff made the house look twice as big. Fortunately, the paint and carpets were in good shape, so a good cleaning was all that was needed before the home went on the MLS.

Donna was unable to do any serious cleaning so they hired a professional cleaning service to clean the house, carpets, and even the windows. Afterwards, it felt like a different house, and even the owners were amazed at the results. It was $700 well spent.

But the big payoff came three days later when a couple who had looked at the home previously went through again. They were astonished at the difference and made a full-price offer. Later at closing, the buyers admitted they were reluctant to go through the second time, but their agent assured them the house was totally different from the first time they saw it.

So Where Do You Start?

First, start with the easy stuff and work from there. Let Figure 10-1 guide you to an exciting world where less is more and homes sell faster.

Neutral Is Good

Many sellers get indignant when an agent makes decluttering suggestions. The agent usually has to patiently explain that the way you live in a house needs to change when you put it on the market. It must be transformed into a neutral home as much as possible so the buyers can visualize themselves living in the house and painting and decorating it however they fancy. It must be like a blank canvas to an artist.

Admittedly, it is possible you'll strike it lucky and get a couple who comes through and loves your pumpkin-colored walls and green carpet. When this happens, the result can be a quick, full-price offer. Maybe this is because you and the buyers live in parallel universes or were born under the same sign. But for whatever reason, they identify with your home on an emotional level first, then justify the dollars-and-cents part later. This is why buyers are sometimes willing to stretch to qualify for a higher price than they originally wanted to go.

After you've decluttered the home and have a few years' worth of accumulation piled high in the garage or an extra room, how about a garage sale? Moving is expensive, and the more you can sell the less you'll have to move. The next section shows how to put together money-making garage sales.

How to Hold Profitable Garage Sales

Whether you've bought a home, sold a home, or both, the cold, harsh reality of moving means that you have to make some hard choices. Take Earl and Shirley, who sold their home they had lived in for twenty-seven years and bought a motor home. The only possible way they could get rid of the mountain of "stuff" they had accumulated over the years was have a garage sale.

In their case it was several garage sales over three weeks. During the week they would pull stuff out of the nooks and crannies of their house, garage, and storage shed and get it ready for sale on weekends.

Luckily, they had a lot of help from some accomplished garage sale

FIGURE 10-1	
Decluttering guide.	
Items (Stuff)	**Suggestions**
Children's Toys	Keep in bins or boxes out of sight.
Old Furniture You No Longer Use	Trash old furniture or donate to charity.
Good Furniture You Want to Keep	Keep only a minimum of furniture in each room, such as a sofa, a chair, and a lamp table or two. Put excess furniture in storage.
Big Entertainment Centers	If they dominate the room, remove and store. It's only for a week or two until the home sells.
Clutter in the Garage or Basement	After decluttering the house with garage sales, moving items into storage, and carting things to good will stores, don't forget the garage and basement. Cleaning and painting the garage walls and floor is a good investment. A sharp, clean garage has made the difference in many sales. Likewise, tidying up the basement is important to a good impression.
Pictures	Keep only one or two pictures on each wall as accent pieces. You want the buyers to imagine their pictures on the wall and not be distracted by your Leroy Nieman collection.
Trophies	Granted, trophies come hard won with sweat, tears, and big bucks. But you want the buyer to imagine her prom queen photo on the mantle and not be distracted by your world-class yellowfin tuna mount. Sorry, everything in this category goes to the storage unit.
Kitchen	Nothing on the counters. No coffee machines, appliances, utensils, radios, TVs, or cookbooks. Also no magnets, calendars, or school work on the refrigerator.

veterans. Here's how they made thousands of dollars and had a lot of fun.

The first step is decide what you want to or must get rid of. If you're moving into a motor home or condo, that means just about everything. To help motivate you: Remember the more you sell, the more money you make and the less you have to pack. The less you have to move, the cheaper it is. You win two ways.

How to Decide What to Sell

Rule number one: If you haven't used it in the past year (some experts say six months), add it to the sales table. Why spend money moving it to your new home if you haven't been using it?

Rule number two: Don't try to predict what people will buy, just add it to the sales pile. One woman who had never thrown away a pair of shoes in twenty years, put out four dozen pairs under pressure from her husband. She was amazed to sell three dozen pairs in two hours.

The goal is to turn as much stuff into cash as you can. What you don't sell you can donate to charity the day before the moving van arrives.

Rule number three: The more stuff you have to sell, the more people will come. So, you may want to get neighbors, friends, relatives, or anyone you can get to join in your garage sale. Perhaps, you can get your neighborhood, cul-de-sac, or even the whole subdivision to join. Many subdivisions and even small towns have yearly garage sales/flea markets that attract thousands of bargain hunters.

How to Price Items for Sale

After deciding what to sell, pricing is the second hardest task most people have in organizing their sale. But the thought of paying big bucks to move an item should temper the urge to keep it. Still, it's important not to project your sentimental attachment on to the pricing of an item.

For furniture, start by estimating what an item would sell for new and then discount it by 75 percent. For example, the leather sofa that you bought nine years ago for $700 would get a price sticker of $175—or less if it's not in good shape.

Assume buyers are knowledgeable and know values. The reason they come to your garage sale is to find a bargain. In bargain hunters' psychology, if you price one item too high and a buyer spots it, she will think everything is priced too high. For old stereo systems, record players, and other obsolete electronics price way down, say to under $30. If you don't sell them there's no other market and they'll end up in your give-away pile in a day or two. They may even make good loss leaders to keep buyers looking around. "The longer they stay, the more they buy"—that's the sales song of veteran garage sellers.

For example, Earl and Shirley found several cases of old but still good Ivory soap bars in a corner of their basement. They put those on a small table priced at fifteen cents a bar with a ten-bars-per-person maximum. The purpose was to get the bargain hunters' juices flowing in anticipation of finding other good bargains.

Clothing items are usually priced in the $1.50 to $5.00 range, and used shoes and sandals sell best when priced at less than $3.00 a pair. Don't sell clothing that is damaged, dirty, stained, or torn—it can hurt your credibility.

Hang the best quality clothing on a rack, and use the price tag to call attention to the brand or original cost. For instance, you could write: *Eddie Bauer leather jacket. $250 new, now only $45.* For lesser value items loose on a table, an effective pricing strategy to increase sales volume can be: *$3.00 each, or 3 for $7.*

Another profitable pricing gambit is selling tools, fishing tackle, or anything you can display individually, as single units. For example, instead of selling a tool box full of tools, sell each tool separately, and instead of a tackle box full of lures, sell each lure for 25 or 50 cents. This can up your profit considerably on high demand items.

How to Advertise Your Garage Sale

The keys to a great garage sale are timing and advertising. To attract the greatest number of people you need to time the sale so the most people possible will come. A warm sunny weekend day is your first choice. If you live in Seattle, that may not be possible, so you may want to consider using your garage or renting a tent to keep everything dry.

The next step is to determine when most people in your area get paid. If it's the first and fifteenth, schedule the sale as close to those dates as possible. You don't want to have your sale around a holiday or weekend if something is happening that will siphon off potential buyers.

The best days are Friday, Saturday, and Sunday. Friday is a good day to start because you'll attract buyers who work on weekends. It's surprising how many people hit the garage sales first thing on Friday morning. Of course, Saturday and Sunday will usually attract the most shoppers. Good times to run the sale are from 8:00 A.M. to 6:00 P.M. on Saturday and from 9:00 A.M. to 4:00 P.M. on Sunday, or as long as shoppers are coming by. Check the newspapers in your area to see what times are most popular. If everyone else is starting at 9:00 A.M., try starting at 8:00 or 8:30 to get them to come to your event first.

Advertising your sale is critical to getting the most shoppers possible. First, determine which papers carry the most garage-sale advertising and run your ads in those. Don't forget the local weeklies and the penny-saver publications with stands around the area. The bargain junkies you want to attract look at these local publications for good deals and upcoming sales. Newsletters from companies, churches, and other organizations are also great options for advertising.

Putting up fliers at work and around the area is effective. Start a week before the sale to get maximum effect.

How to Drive Bargain Hunters into a Feeding Frenzy

The bigger the sale, the more stuff shoppers have to look at, so size is a dominant feature you'll want to include in your ads. Use phrases such as "large neighborhood, 15 house, multiple house, area-wide" to convey how big the sale will be. Next, draw the reader in by giving a few tantalizing examples of demand items for your area. List examples, such as baby clothes, patio furniture, specific appliances, tools, sporting goods, and furniture.

Also important is giving clear and precise directions on how to get there. Make liberal use of landmarks, such as turn left at the Longmont Burger King, or one block south of Middleville Safeway. Also provide the date and times, but don't list your phone number. You want them to come by, not call you.

For example, here's an ad for an estate sale that pulled hundreds of bargain hunters:

Moving/Estate Sale

362 E. Lupine Cir.
Turn N. at Burger King on Shepard Ln. and follow signs.

Nothing thrown away in 30 years. Furniture, appliances, books, tools, kitchenware, freezer, you name it.

Everything must go including house.

Sale Friday & Saturday 7 A.M. to 3 P.M.

At 7:00 A.M. the morning of the sale the line was long and people were waiting impatiently. Sales were frantic all morning and into the late afternoon, well past the advertised end.

What made this ad work so well? The words estate or moving sale are always powerful. That everything was up for sale including the house was also a compelling draw. And undoubtedly, the mental image of a house full of thirty-years' worth of collected stuff for sale stirred bargain hunters' imaginations.

Best of all, a couple of days later the house—nearly empty by now—also sold because of the publicity and activity generated by the garage sale.

Directional Signs Are a Must

Another important tool for bringing in buyers are directional signs, the more the better. These signs can be simple, with the words Garage Sale and an arrow. Many home centers sell these signs with wire frames that stick into the ground.

Put signs at all intersections within a two-block radius and roads that feed into your area. Attaching balloons or flags will make them even more visible. Realtors often use balloons tied to their open-house signs to add to their visibility and it works.

Printing the garage-sale information on brightly colored index cards and sticking them around the area on bulletin boards, telephone poles, or wherever you can also helps draw attention to your sale.

You can also buy strings of brightly colored plastic flags in 50 ft to 100 ft lengths that will add considerably to the visibility of your site.

How to Set Up the Sales Site

A day or two before the sale, price tag everything so there's no question what the prices are. Use tags or masking tape with the price written on with a black marker. A good shortcut is putting $1 items on one table, $2 items on another table, and so on.

Next, spread the goods out as much as possible. Make it easy for shoppers to walk around tables and see what you've got. Put the best goods in front so drive-bys can see this is a sale worth stopping at.

Make sure clothes are clean, pressed, and on hangers. If you have a lot of kids' clothes, bag and label several same-size items for $x a bag.

Have a table up front with tools, camping gear, golf clubs, and fishing stuff to attract the male drive-bys. Likewise, package a few toys in plastic bags to sell to the kids for 10 to 25 cents to keep them happy and the parents around longer.

If you have appliances, run an extension cord to a table so buyers can make sure everything works before buying.

Also important is to have a supply of small bills and lots of change since garage sales are a cash business. Have at least twenty $1 bills, five $5 bills, five $10 bills, and two $20 bills. For change, get a roll of quarters, dimes, and nickels. Having a metal cash box with compartments for coins and bills will save you a lot of time. Don't accept credit cards unless you're set up for it and can process the transactions on the spot. And absolutely no checks, no exceptions.

Finally, make sure you have enough parking. Let the neighbors know what's happening and thank them for being cooperative afterwards. Good will is always important.

Preparing Your Stuff for Sale

It's a good idea to make your stuff look as good as possible. Clean, repair, and polish everything so it looks its best. First impressions often make the difference between a sale and a reject.

Also make the tables as neat and attractive as possible. This often means constant effort to keep them that way, but it's worth it. A well-organized site gives shoppers the confidence to look a little longer and buy more.

Negotiating Tips

Many people hesitate to have garage sales because they aren't comfortable dealing with shoppers or lack confidence in their negotiating ability. The first step in overcoming these doubts is realize that it's not a matter of win or lose. You want to sell and the buyer wants to buy. It's like a friendly chat over coffee. You bat the price back and forth in a friendly way until you both agree and it's a done deal.

True, 95 percent of garage-sale shoppers will want to talk you down; after all, they're bargain hunters, and they're there to get the best deal they can. You know that so you anticipate it and plan for it.

Garage Sale Web Sites
www.yardsalesupplies.com
www.garagesaletools.com
www.yardsailor.com
www.gsonly.com
www.insiderreports.com

One technique is to price your goods a little high so you can come down. For example, if you have a lamp that you feel will sell for $10, price it at $15 so the buyer will feel she got a bargain by talking you down. If you reach an impasse, offer to split the difference. She offers $8, you counter with $12, and then you offer to split the difference at $10. Many shoppers will go along with that.

Remember that if you keep it friendly, don't get too serious, and don't forget it's not a win-lose contest, you'll have a lot of profitable fun.

It's even more fun to tap into a huge garage sale where the whole planet can shop, the Internet. Using eBay, you can connect with people who avidly collect just about anything.

Selling Stuff on E-Bay

Before you put collectibles on the Internet, you'll need to organize the information. First, take digital photos of the items and save them to a file. It's helpful to create and label a new folder that contains only the photos of what you're offering for sale.

You don't have to buy a digital camera if you don't have one. Most photo processors can put your pictures on a disk in JPEG format that's commonly used to paste photos on the Internet.

Number each photo as you save the data from your camera or disk to the new folder. After you've downloaded the photos, create another file in that folder, key in descriptions of what you're selling, and number them so they correspond to the photo numbers. This is so once you're in eBay you can cut and paste the descriptions rather than type them in when you're online.

Even though eBay allows one photo per item free, they'll require a credit card number to bill you in case you want to add additional views on an item.

You'll also have a choice of time limits for bidding. Many veteran eBay sellers suggest that you go the seven-day option because activity is heavier on weekends. Traffic just before your bidding time limit expires also tends to be heavy.

How to Make Sales Go Smoothly

A great way to handle the payment is to use Paypal (*www.paypal.com*). This is a third party that collects the funds for you by credit card or electronic funds transfer. They release the money to you when cleared and you ship to the buyer as arranged.

Some tips to make the sales go smoothly are:

■ Quote a price for the item only and mention in the remarks that shipping will be extra.

■ You may want to disclose the weight of an item if it will make a difference in how it's shipped.

- If possible, quote approximate handling and shipping charges. The buyer may have a preference on how they want an item shipped, however.

- If you're selling your home, the best time to start this process is several months before you put it on the market. Getting your home ready to sell, holding garage sales, and other demands on your time during the actual sale period can create a big time crunch if you have too many projects going at once.

Garage sales, eBay, and selling your home can create a whirlwind of activity over several months, culminating in the actual moving, which can be the most stressful. To minimize the costs and avoid being taken, the next section will give some tips on finding a good mover and getting on the road.

How to Find and Work with Movers

Moving is one of those fun experiences both buyers and sellers are going to experience soon after closing. The moving industry has taken a lot of heat lately from the media over a few bad apples taking advantage of consumers. And the truth is when it comes to choosing a mover, it's definitely buyer beware.

Because moving companies generally can charge what they want, it pays to shop around for not only the best price, but for a mover that'll get you there in one piece.

Consider these tips when you shop for a mover:

- Start by asking friends, coworkers, and your Realtor for names of movers they've had a good experience with. Get a list of at least six companies. Check to see if they're a member of the American Moving and Storage Association (AMSA), a trade group that arranges arbitration to settle disputes.

- Narrow down your list to the best three and check the Better Business Bu-

Websites Worth Checking Out

www.amconf.org

www.movingadvocateam .com

www.monstermoving.com

www.homestore.com/ move

www.move.com

www.moving.org

www.buyboxes.com

www.usps.gov/moversnet

www.makethemove.com

www.helpumove.com

www.bbb.org

(Better Business Bureau)

reau for complaints. Eliminate any who have had more than one or two the past year. Also ask the moving companies if they have any contracts with corporate relocation departments. Call the references to see if the contract is still active and if there have been any complaints.

■ Next, call the remaining movers on your list and request a walk-through and a written estimate. Ask if the bid is binding or nonbinding. A binding bid may come in higher, but it discourages a mover from jacking up the price on moving day when they know you're under a lot of pressure.

■ Ask lots of questions and make sure you understand how the movers calculate their charges. Typically a mover charges by weight and distance, although in-state moves are often charged according to the number of man-hours it'll take to get the job done. Look out for other charges, such as for having the mover buy and pack the boxes, which can run up the bill big time.

■ Review the bids to see if there are extra charges for packing materials, travel time, or whatever. Don't be bashful negotiating these fees down. The moving business is a competitive industry and they want your business.

Appliance Life Span

To help you decide whether it is worth paying to move your appliance, consider these average life expectancies.

Refrigerator, 11–13 years

Electric dryer, 11–13 years

Washing machine, 10–12 years

Microwave, 9–11 years

Iron, 7–9 years

Mixer, 7–9 years

Toaster, 6–8 years

Coffee maker, 3–6 years

■ Most moving companies include standard insurance coverage as part of their bid. However, the coverage is for only 60 cents a pound. That means if your 70-pound wide-screen flat panel HDTV you paid $2,100 for gets dropped, you'll get paid $42 for it. That makes it almost mandatory to get additional coverage through your insurance company or the mover. Full replacement coverage gives the best protection and is also the most expensive. Of course, you'll want to shop around and compare rates.

■ Many savvy consumers let their movers handle the appliances, large boxes, and furniture, and they pack and transport the smaller valuable things themselves, even to the extent of renting a small trailer.

■ If there's an insurance claim you'll need to show proof that you owned the item. A good way to document this is keep a file of serial numbers and purchase receipts. Then photo or videotape the items going onto the moving van. A tape or CD with images of everything important taken prior to and just after loading can back up a claim if your widescreen HDTV gets broken.

■ Make sure the mover knows how to contact you at the destination to schedule delivery. If you can't be reached, your goods may go into storage with additional charges tacked on.

Timing Your Move Can Save You Money

May to September are moving companies' busiest months. School is out, and many people want to move and get settled in before school starts again. If you can avoid these months, you'll usually get better rates and service.

Similarly, many people need to move at the beginning or the end of the month because mortgage and rent payments generally fall on the first. If you can schedule your move in the middle of month, your chances of getting better service and exact moving dates are better.

Book your moving date at least six weeks in advance. Waiting until the last minute sets you up for higher prices and shoddy service.

Moving-Related Tax Deductions

Moving for most people is high on the list of painful activities. But, if you can squeeze a tax deduction out of the process it may help a little. Not everyone can deduct their moving expenses. The IRS rules that guide deductions for moving expenses are complicated, so it's important to check with a tax professional.

Generally, the IRS will allow deductions if the move is job related and is 50 miles or more away from the old employment.

If your job-related move qualifies, you may be able to write off the moving company's entire bill, including packing costs and any charges for storing household goods within 30 days of relocation. Other possible write-offs are one-way travel expenses to your new house. Travel expenses can add up, and if you qualify, you can get a hefty tax break that year.

> For information on deducting moving expenses, get IRS publication 521, *Moving Expenses,* at 800-829-1040 or go to *www.irs.gov.*

Why Home Values Increase

Real estate values are a function of supply and demand, which in turn are influenced by interest rates, the local and national economy, and changing demographics. When interest rates drop—especially to historic lows as they have recently—it allows more people to qualify for a mortgage.

As a result, mortgage lenders, Realtors, and builders aggressively market homes, and demand mushrooms. Renters decide now is the time to fire the landlord and soon more buyers are chasing a finite number of homes for sale.

At first, buyers find they have to offer full price or more to have a chance of getting a home, and multiple offers become the norm. Soon every time a home goes on the market it's a littler higher than a similar one down the street that sold last month.

Randy and Bernie experienced this when they sold their home they had lived in for six years. They bought the home in 1998 for $280,000 and sold it in 2004 for $463,000. Thanks to a good location and warming housing market, their home appreciated 65.4 percent, or an average of about 11 percent per year.

It gets even more exciting when you consider that the true return on investment is computed on the down payment, not the purchase price. For example, when Randy and Bernie bought their home they wrote out a check for $39,200 for down payment and closing costs. Six years later their investment had grown to $183,000, or a gain of 367 percent! The financial types who crunch numbers call this leverage.

Factors That Make a Home Increase in Value

When several value-enhancing factors—such as proximity to good schools, shopping, or a short commute—enter the picture, home prices will skyrocket. Sometimes only a single factor, such as having a university close by or a demographics change where young professionals move into an older area and start fixing up homes, can send values up.

Obviously, the more enhancing factors that affect an area, the bigger the value increase. Some enhancing factors are location, the neighborhood, and the economy.

Location

Not surprisingly, at the top of the value food chain is location. Some common factors that make a good location are:

- Schools that are perceived better or more desirable than the norm

- Upscale shopping close by

- Good access to freeways, but yet far enough away to avoid noise and congestion

- Proximity to a university or cultural centers

- Well-kept neighborhoods with charming architectural styles

- Low crime rate

If you bought your home a few years ago and the area has changed for the better, your investment has most likely grown considerably.

This happened to Phil and Marie when they sold a small red-brick bungalow they bought as a fixer-upper four years ago. Their house, like others in the area, was built in the 1950s, and the tree-lined streets attracted mostly first-time home buyers. Then a large regional medical center was built close by, the influx of people to the area revitalized the small business district nearby, and home values begin to go up. People who worked at the medical center, and at the increasing number of businesses now attracted to the area, wanted to live close by. As a result of supply and demand, the home market exploded.

Phil and Marie bought their home for $87,000 and invested another $32,000 upgrading the kitchen, furnace, and adding central air. They also spent countless hours stripping layers of old wallpaper, and restoring the woodwork and wood floors. When they were ready to sell, the home's value had rocketed to $212,000. Adding the cost of improvements to the purchase price netted a 78-percent value increase in four years. As the saying goes, the rising tide lifts all boats.

Phil and Marie's house buying experience could also have turned out differently. Suppose a freeway expansion project put an on/off ramp nearby instead of a medical center. Rather than enhancing the area, the ramp would likely trigger a slow decline in house values. There would be nothing upscale to attract home buyers willing to pay top dollar to live there.

The bottom line on location is that if your area is on the upswing you'll profit, and time is on your side. On the other hand, if the area is stagnant or declining, then selling is your best option. There's not much you can do to increase your home's value, and any money you spend on upgrades will likely be wasted. It boils down to a small loss now being better than a bigger loss later on.

The Neighborhood

Next in importance to location is the neighborhood. The condition of other homes in your area has a big impact on your home's value. If you've added improvements that make your home the best on the block, it can cost you. On the flip side, if all the other homes are bigger or in better condition than yours, you'll benefit.

It's also true that neighborhoods can change and improve. For example, there may be streets of older homes that have not been taken care of because the original owners have moved and where the current owners lack a pride of ownership in the area. If there are no big negatives to stand in the way, a growing population will rediscover the area and it can become trendy again.

When local governments take an interest in an area, homes can explode in value, as, for example, when previous negatives such as old factories or mill sites are converted into upscale shopping malls, medical centers, new subdivisions, or convention centers.

Also not to be ignored is the impact of schools on an area. If the neighborhood schools have a reputation for excellence, a home's value can go up by several thousand dollars. It's a matter of supply and demand because not all the parents who want their kids to go to a certain school can buy within the boundaries. As a result, a home can sell for a few thousand dollars more than one across the street that's just outside the school's boundaries.

Economic Factors

When interest rates drop it's like discounting home prices. Mortgage payments become more competitive with rentals and demand increases. This puts pressure on entry-level and mid-level homes, so prices ratchet up.

In turn, sellers of entry-level homes usually take their big equity gains and move up to more expensive homes. New-home construction explodes and prices up and down the spectrum go up. This is what happened the last few years as low interest rates fueled demand in most areas. In some urban areas already experiencing heavy growth, the low interest rates caused the housing market to explode, and entry-level homes soared into the $200,000 to $400,000 price level.

In some areas of the country, homes have appreciated dramatically the last few years. If you were to sell and move from a high appreciation area like San Francisco to a lower appreciation area like North Dakota, your equity and the same monthly payment could allow you to buy a significantly larger home.

Tony and Mariela found this out when they moved from Orange County, California, to Salt Lake City, Utah. Five years ago in California, they had put $16,000 down and took out a $304,000 mortgage on a 2,900 square-foot three-bedroom, two-bath ranch. When they recently sold their home for $469,000, they profited $152,200 after selling expenses. Buying a similar home in Utah they found would cost them approximately $195,000.

However, if Tony and Mariela had moved from Utah to California they would have gotten a bad case of sticker shock. At the same price and monthly payment they had before, they would probably have been able to afford only a one-bedroom loft or condo.

Although the national economy strongly influences local real estate, the equity you accrue is still dependent on local supply and demand. When you cash out your equity and move to another area, you'll most likely get either a housing upgrade or suffer sticker shock.

This economic reality also applies to renting. Moving from an apartment in Fargo, North Dakota, to New York City would also give you a severe case of sticker shock. Also, as a renter you wouldn't even have any equity from your last house to cushion you.

APPENDIX B

Features That Affect Marketing Time and Selling Price

☐ The overall area and neighborhood are the two most important considerations for not only how fast a home will sell, but what the sales price will be. How does your home compare with others in the neighborhood?

☐ How does your home appear to people driving by or getting out of their car (curb appeal)?
   1. Does the home fit in with other homes in the neighborhood?
   2. Is the landscaping attractive and will it encourage buyers to explore further?
   3. Does the walkway build anticipation of what's to come?
   4. Is the front entryway attractive and does it convey the promise that the rest of the home is in equally good condition?
   5. Is the walkway to the front door well lighted?

☐ How does the home's interior stack up to the competition?
   1. Is the inside entryway bright and inviting with light, neutral paint?
   2. How about the floors? Are floor coverings clean and in good shape? Do wood floors need to be sanded and refinished?
   3. Are the kitchen cabinets in good condition?
   4. Do the counters need replacing with new colors or finishes?

    5. Are the bathrooms updated and in good condition? How about the caulking around tubs and showers?

    6. Are the bedrooms' paint and floor coverings in good shape?

☐ How are the appliances and mechanical systems?

    1. Are the kitchen appliances in good condition and do the colors match?

    2. Is the water heater in good condition with no leaks?

    3. Has the heating system been checked and serviced recently and do you have a copy of the paperwork to show that it's been done?

    4. Is the air conditioning system in good shape and has it been recently checked?

    5. If your lawn has a sprinkling system, are the heads and lines working with no leaks?

☐ What about your home's exterior?

    1. If the roof is still under warranty, do you have the paperwork to show a buyer? Also, if your home is older, can you verify when the roof was replaced?

    2. Is the siding in good condition with no peeling paint and no dented aluminum or vinyl panels?

    3. How about the downspouts and gutters?

    4. Is the driveway (concrete, asphalt, or gravel) in good shape? Is there a parking space for RVs?

Marketing Do's and Don'ts

After you've gotten your home in great selling shape, use this list to check all the things you need to do to let everyone know your home is on the market.

☐ Plant as many signs as needed so drive-bys can see your phone number from all directions.

☐ Have one large phone number on the sign so people can see it at a glance as they drive by. If you have a cell phone use that number so you are always in touch.

☐ Don't clutter up your sign with any other information other than the phone number. Few people will stop and squint at the small print. The details go on the flier.

☐ Put a brochure box next to the sign and keep it stocked with fliers. See Chapter 3 for flier-writing tips.

☐ Make sure everyone on your street and the surrounding streets gets a flier. Also, put them up on any bulletin boards in the area.

☐ Don't let anyone who stops by go through the home without an appointment. Especially, don't show the home when you're alone. Always have a family member or neighbor present when buyers come through.

☐ See Chapter 3 for ad-writing tips.

☐ Ads run in weeklies tend to have a longer shelf life than dailies and are usually less expensive and more effective.

☐ Hold open houses on weekends. Use lots of directional signs to guide people.

☐ Have a folder handy with utility bills, warranties, inspections, and comparable properties that have sold or are for sale in the area. Buyers will be impressed that you're prepared and have important data at your fingertips.

☐ If you have an interested buyer make sure they've been to the bank and are preapproved for a loan. Always call their lender and verify everything even if they have a preapproval letter.

☐ Don't put your home on the market before you have a place to live. You don't want to get caught like a deer in the headlights if an offer comes in with a short closing deadline and you don't have a place lined up.

Do's and Don'ts When You Get an Offer

When an offer comes in, use this checklist to make sure you don't miss anything vital that can cost you.

☐ First, the offer must be in writing or it's no more than superheated air. That applies to the purchase agreement and any addendums. If it's not in writing, it doesn't exist.

☐ Number all addendums in consecutive order. Lenders get upset when there are missing addendums or pages.

☐ Make sure all addendums and counter offers have a short response deadline written in. You don't want your offers or counter offers shopped or used to leverage a better offer from another interested buyer.

☐ Don't get emotional and take low offers personally. Many buyers make a low offer assuming you'll counter up to your lowest price. The buyers may love the home and may be scared they'll lose it, but someone may have told them this is the way to buy a home.

☐ If you get a low offer, counter back slightly higher than your bottom line. Give yourself a little room in case they come back with a counter-counter offer. Also, don't assume that price is all you have to work with. Adding appliances, yard equipment, or paint and carpet allowances can often make the deal work.

☐ Offering an extended or shorter closing date or a rent-back for a couple of months can sometimes make the deal work.

☐ Make sure that all appliances, blinds, drapes, rugs, etc., that are to be included with the sale are listed on the purchase contract or addendum. It's also important to list on the paperwork all excluded items, such as an antique chandelier, portable microwave oven, and so on.

☐ Make up a list of the contract deadlines and what the offer is subject to. It's important to stay on top of these dates because missing one date can void the offer. Typical examples of deadlines are disclosures of lead-based-paint and property-condition.

What Your Ads Need to Attract Quality Buyers: Checklist

☐ Buyers skim the ads looking for trigger words that grab their attention, and you want to use these words in the headline. Effective trigger words are usually the following:
1. The subdivision name if your home is in a sought-after area
2. High-demand schools and their proximity
3. Your home's architectural style if that's a big demand item
4. Anything that makes your home stand out from the crowd or is in big demand

☐ Always include the price. You want to attract those who can afford your home, not curious lookers.

☐ List the square footage, number of bedrooms and baths, and whether the basement is finished. The year built or remodeled is also important.

☐ Describe a view, proximity to a park, or other desirable features.

☐ Avoid abbreviations and unfamiliar terms.

☐ List your cell phone number if you have one. Make it easy for buyers to contact you. Don't use an answering machine or voice mail unless you absolutely have to.

APPENDIX F

How to Avoid the Seven Costliest Mistakes Homeowners Make

Mistake #1: Putting the House on the Market Before It's Ready

An all-too-common mistake home sellers make is simply pound a *For Sale* sign in the turf and wait for someone to write them a check. True, this approach sometimes brings an offer, but how many thousands of dollars does the seller lose when they could have gotten more?

To sell a home for the most money, it has to be properly marketed. Like anything else in sales, it's the packaging that brings in bigger bucks.

In one example of packaging, a couple had tried to sell their home for three months. They had shown it many times, and no one had made an offer. People would walk through quickly and leave, often without pausing to ask questions or make comments.

The sellers were clueless. They felt all they had to do was put a sign in the yard and the home would sell. But, after three months they started to panic and called Lori, an agent their neighbor recommended.

Walking through the home, the agent could see why the home wasn't selling. It was obvious. The oak floors were dull and scuffed and the walls needed paint badly. Appliances, boxes, and dishes covered the kitchen counters and the chipped sink was full of dirty dishes. The rest of the house was in similar condition. It wasn't a home anyone would want to buy unless they were looking for a fixer-upper.

Lori sat down with the sellers and worked up a "to do" list of repairs that would make the house attractive and saleable. However, the sellers refused to do the items on the list. They just wanted to sell as-is and get out of town.

When Lori couldn't get the sellers to budge on doing the repairs, she told them she couldn't help them and walked away from a potential listing. She had learned the hard way before about trying to sell a "junker" property for market value.

Long story short, when the sellers couldn't sell the home, they rented it and moved several states away. About two months after that, the renters skipped out and left an even bigger mess. Eventually, the home went into foreclosure and the sellers lost about $40,000 in equity and took a big ding on their credit.

Although this is an extreme case, there are vital lessons we can glean from this example that can help you avoid costly mistakes:

■ If you want to sell your home "as-is," market your home to fixer-upper or investor buyers. They usually pay cash (no appraisers, no bank rules) but at a heavily discounted price. You'll get a lot more money if you fix it up first.

Also, a home has to be appraised, and if the appraiser comes back with a list of repairs, you're back where you started. It's best to invest time and money putting the home in good selling condition first. You'll usually get the money you spent in repairs back plus a lot more.

■ Look around the neighborhood and see what other homeowners have done. You want your home to look just a tad better. Buyers buy into a neighborhood first, and if your home fits in you'll attract the buyer who pays at or close to list price.

■ Don't try and cut corners by offering a painting or carpeting allowance. If your home needs paint and floor coverings, buyers will frequently make low offers and want the allowance as well.

■ Once buyers find something wrong, their thinking goes into "what else is wrong" mode, and any offers will be for "how low can we get the house for."

■ As mentioned in the beginning chapters, most people buy homes on emotion. The more you appeal to their emotions, the less price becomes an issue. If your home is the buyer's dream home, you'll likely get a full-price offer.

Mistake #2: Overimproving the Home for the Neighborhood

Just the opposite of putting your home on the market "as-is" is improving it more than other homes in the area. This creates a "white elephant" in real estate speak.

This situation often happens when homeowners feel they're going to live in the home forever and therefore any improvements they do is okay. Unfortunately, forever is now less than seven years, the average time a homeowner stays in a home before moving. If a job change, transfer, or a move to be closer to family happens, selling for what you've got invested in the home becomes difficult.

Typically, homeowners run into these problems when they do any of the following:

1. Adding on to the home and it becomes bigger than others in the neighborhood.

2. Using more expensive materials in remodeling or upgrading, such as expensive imported tile in place of vinyl, or granite countertops when the area norm is laminate.

3. On the exterior, installing a tile or slate roof when all the other homes have asphalt shingles, or using brick when vinyl siding is the norm.

4. If no one else in your area has a swimming pool, tennis court, or trout pond, and you put one in, it's almost certain you won't get your investment back. In these cases it's often better to sell your home and buy one in an area that will support your improvement. It gets even stickier if you're overimproved, have to sell, and your mortgage is more than the home's market value. This can easily happen because many mortgage lenders loan up to 125 percent of appraisal, especially on second loans.

Here's some suggestions on how you can avoid overimproving for the area:

■ First, look at what other homeowners have done in improvements and upgrades and stay close to what they've done. True, this can rankle rugged individualists who don't like a "me too" approach. But the hard fact still remains that if you want a bigger or better home, you'll need to find a neighborhood that will support it if you want to maintain your investment.

■ If you refinance, be careful that lenders don't give you an inflated appraisal and loan you more than the home is worth. You can avoid this by looking at what similar homes have sold for the last couple of months.

■ Go through open houses and homes for sale in your area and see what other owners have done. Notice which homes sell quickly and which ones don't.

■ If your area is not going up in value, you won't want to do more to the home than keep it in good condition.

Mistake #3: Pricing the Home Based on What You Want to Net

When Brett and Julie put their home on the market they took their mortgage balance, and then added in estimated closing costs and the $60,000 they needed to get into their next home, which they were having built. Totaling up these figures they came up with $347,000 for a sale price. With a lot of hope, they planted a *For Sale* sign in the lawn, put an ad in the local paper, and sat back to see what would happen.

The first weekend went by and nothing happened. After three more weekends with only a couple of lookers, the sellers felt they had better talk to a Realtor. Time was getting short and their new home would be finished in two months.

The agent sat down with Brett and Julie and went over what other similar homes had sold for in their area the last couple of months. Those comparisons showed that similar homes sold for between $315,000 to $325,000, with an average sales time of 73 days. Also, looking at comparable homes currently for sale showed 27 listings in a mile radius. That meant the seller's home had a lot of competition.

By looking at what homes had sold for and factoring in the large number of homes currently for sale, the Realtor suggested a sales price of $319,900. This was $27,100 less than the sellers needed to get. Plus, they had only 60 days until their new home would be finished.

So what happened? Brett and Julie, upset over the dash of cold reality, cancelled their build job with the builder and lost their $8,000 deposit. Their qualifying ratios were so tight that without a net $60,000 from the sale of their home, they couldn't buy the new one.

To avoid making this type of pricing problem on your home, you can:

1. Have a Realtor pull up a list of what similar homes have sold for in your area the last few months. Note the list prices, actual sales prices, and number of days on the market.

2. Look at what similar homes to yours are priced at in your area.

3. Pay a few hundred dollars and hire a certified appraiser. For Brett and Julie, this would have been far cheaper than losing their deposit.

Mistake #4: Not Hiring an Agent Based on Merit or Track Record

Not many people would consider letting friends or relatives work on their $60,000 Lexus unless they were factory-trained mechanics. Yet, it's amazing how many homeowners don't think twice about entrusting their $350,000 home to a friend or relative who may have just gotten a real estate license.

The skills needed to sell your home for the most money and ensure the transaction goes smoothly is developed through years of education and experience. Not choosing a professional agent with a good track record can have the same results as hiring an untrained person in any other field: It can cost you money, frustration, and stress.

So how do you find a competent agent?

1. Start by asking those who have recently sold homes how they liked their agent, just as you would if you wanted to find a good mechanic, electrician, or tax accountant.

2. Especially beware of unprofessional agents who tell you that your home is worth more than it is in order to get a listing. These agents will not only be back in a couple of weeks wanting a price reduction, but you may be stuck with an unscrupulous agent until the listing runs out.

3. Mortgage lenders, title people, and real estate attorneys see first-hand how good a job an agent does. Ask these people for their recommendations and add the agents to your list.

4. Look for agents who do business in your area. You'll see their signs around. Don't be shy about asking the owners of the homes listed how they like their agent. Add the ones who get good recommendations to your short list.

5. After you've narrowed down your list to three or four agents, give them a call and make appointments to talk.

6. Look for an agent who takes a genuine interest in your situation and just doesn't give you a monologue of how great he or she is and how many homes they've sold.

7. Ask to see MLS printouts of the agent's last ten or more listings. Note on the printout:

- The list price versus sold price.

- How many days the home was on the market.

- The dollar amount of any concessions. (This is not always bad; it can tell you whether the agent knows how to put deals together in a slow market.)

- If the listing hasn't sold, note how long the home has been on the market and whether there have been price reductions along the way.

8. Pick the agent with whom you feel most comfortable.

Mistake #5: Getting Emotionally Involved in the Sale of the Home

Many home sellers make this mistake when they can't see their home objectively. For example, experienced agents constantly run into sellers who say, "We've put a lot into this home, and if the Jones's down the street sold their home for $275,000 then ours should be worth $325,000." These sellers don't realize emotionally that their home is worth what other similar homes have sold for in the area. See mistakes 1 and 2.

The second area where sellers run into problems is in showing their home. Buyers are not always tactful and sometimes they'll bad-mouth the home. This can also be a negotiating strategy. If they can make you believe your home is priced too high they can slip in a low offer.

If you let yourself get upset by such comments it can cloud your ability to work up a successful deal.

A similar situation is a buyer coming in with a low offer. Many sellers take this personally and lose an opportunity to make a sale. If you get a low offer, stay cool and counter up to your best price. It's amazing how often buyers will accept a counter that you didn't think would fly.

Mistake #6: Trying to Cover Up Problems or Not Disclosing Them

Some sellers create huge problems by not disclosing problems with the house. They hope buyers won't find out, but they always do, and a lawsuit can result.

This often happens when the buyer hires a professional inspector, who finds problems the seller has not disclosed. This can kill a promising sale fast because the buyer loses confidence and walks away from the deal. Even when the seller offers to take care of the problems, it's sometimes not enough to rekindle the buyer's interest.

Remember, buyers are emotional people too.

Here are some tips on how to avoid losing a buyer due to disclosure.

1. Fill out your state's disclosure form completely. If in doubt, explain past problems and how they've been taken care of. Use specifics on what caused the problem, what was done about it, and what materials were used.

2. Don't try to sell a house "as-is" to get around problems you know about. You'll have trouble getting financing, and buyers may still come back and sue you.

If the home is a true dump, work with an attorney to put together paperwork that will protect you from future liability.

3. Hire a reputable home inspector (see the yellow pages under "Home Inspectors") to inspect your home before it goes on the market. You can then use the inspection report as a marketing tool. Show buyers up front that the home is in good condition. If the inspector finds problems, fix or replace them and have the report updated. Spending about $300 in the beginning can save big bucks later on in the sales process.

Mistake #7: Not Getting Your Ducks Lined Up Before Trying to Sell

In addition to the problems in mistake 1, sellers often create other situations that cost them money or unnecessary stress. Consider the following situations:

■ For example, one all too common situation sellers create is waiting to put their home on the market when buying a new home so they won't have to move twice. Doing this can cause major stress if the home doesn't sell by closing date for the new home. Many deposits are lost because buyers don't plan ahead.

It's better to give yourself plenty of time to sell the home and line up a rental or a relative to stay with in case your home sells quickly.

■ Check out your mortgage loan and make sure you don't have a prepayment penalty. Many sellers get to closing and find out they have a several-thousand-dollar fee tacked on by the mortgage company for paying off their mortgage early.

■ If you have pets, make arrangements to board them or have a neighbor pet-sit while you're showing the home. You may love your dogs, cats, or tropical snakes, but buyers who don't like animals or have allergies will make a fast U-turn out of the home if your pets are there. It's likely any agent who has sold more than two homes can relate horror stories of pets or pet smells killing potential sales.

■ Don't put your home on the market subject to finding another home. You'll discourage serious buyers from considering your home. Buyers won't want to wait around for you to find another house.

If this is a concern for you and the market is fairly hot, try finding a home and making an offer subject to your home selling. Perhaps the seller of the home you want needs a longer time to move and it could be a win-win. True, this is a weak approach, but it beats discouraging buyers from making offers on your home by putting in conditions.

■ Sometimes there are legal matters—like a divorce, death, liens, judgments, or other problems—that affect title. It's vital to get them completely cleaned up before putting the home on the market.

One particularly vexing problem is when there has been a divorce and the ex's name is still on the title. When the house sells, the ex decides that now is the time for payback and refuses to sign a quit claim deed or whatever is needed to complete the sale. If there's any doubt about clear title, get with an attorney and clean it up before planting the *For Sale* sign.

Glossary

Addendum. An addition or modification to a purchase agreement. Sometimes called a rider or amendment.

Adjustable Rate Mortgage (ARM). A mortgage with a payment that goes up or down according to the performance of an economic index such as the one-year Treasury Bill. Payments can adjust every six months, one year, two years, etc., depending on the plan. The margin (stays constant) is added to the index rate to come up with the interest rate you'll pay for the next adjustment period.

Agency. The relationship between a buyer or seller and a real estate broker.

Allowance. The amount of money a contractor allows for appliances, upgrades, or options.

Amortization. When a loan's monthly payments include principal and interest and will pay to zero in x number of years, it's called an amortized loan. A printout that shows how much goes to principal and interest each month is an amortization schedule.

Annual percentage rate (APR). The APR interest rate is calculated by adding the closing costs to the loan amount and recalculating keeping the payment and term the same.

Application fees. Fees that you pay a lender up front for a credit report, appraisal, and sometimes for locking in an interest rate.

Appraisal. The opinion of a licensed appraiser on what a property is worth in the current market. Appraisers are licensed in most states.

Appreciation. When a home's value increases.

Balloon mortgage. A mortgage that typically has payments of a 30-year mortgage, but with the full balance due much sooner, in 1, 5, or 10 years, for example.

Bid. A written proposal from a contractor to build a house according to the specifications you agree on for a certain price. Also, subcontractors can submit bids for certain parts of the construction.

Building permit. A document issued by the city or county building department granting permission to build the house according to the specs you've submitted.

Buy-down. Typically, a lender will give you a lower interest rate for a fee. For instance, 1 percent of the loan amount could buy down the interest rate 1/6 of 1 percent, depending on the market. Builders can advertise a lower interest because they've agreed to pay the lender for the buy-down.

Buyer's market. Market conditions that favor the buyer. There are more homes for sale than there are buyers. The opposite is a *seller's market*.

Callback. A return visit by the contractor to repair or replace items he has found to be unsatisfactory or that require service under the warranty.

Cap. On a variable interest loan it's the maximum rate a loan can go during the life of the loan.

CC&R. Covenants, conditions, and restrictions are recorded rules that govern what you can and can't do with your property.

Change order. Written authorization for the contractor to make changes or additions to the original contract along with any additional costs incurred.

Closing costs. Fees paid at closing to the lender. They typically total 3–4% of the loan amount.

Closing statement. Also known as a *settlement statement* or *HUD*.

Comparative Market Analysis (CMA). Sometimes known as "comps" in the real estate industry. These are lists of similar properties to yours that have sold and are currently for sale. Agents and appraisers compile comps to help establish what a home should sell for.

Condominium. A dwelling of two or more units where the homeowners own the interior space of their unit but own everything else in common with the other owners.

Conforming loan. One that meets with *Fannie Mae* or *Freddie Mac* underwriting standards.

Conventional mortgage. A mortgage that is not insured by a government agency. Quasi-government corporations like *Fannie Mae* and *Freddie Mac,* as well as banks, pension funds, and investors, buy these loans as investments.

Co-op building. An apartment building that is owned by a corporation that sells shares to people who want to lease an apartment.

Owning shares entitles you to lease a certain apartment, and you pay a monthly assessment, which includes your share of operating costs and taxes.

Cost-plus contract. You agree to pay the contractor the cost of materials and labor plus a certain percentage for profit and overhead. This is also known as a time and materials contract.

Counteroffer. When you make a written offer on property, the sellers can accept, reject, or counter your offer with the price and/or terms they will agree to in writing. Sometimes, the counter, counteroffer process goes back and forth several times until the parties reach agreement.

Curb appeal. The impression a house gives when a buyer drives by to assess the property.

Depreciation. When a home's value decreases.

Desktop underwriting. Automated underwriting.

Discount broker. A broker who is willing to list your home for a reduced commission or a flat fee.

Draw. A payment to the contractor at certain stages of construction to pay for work done to that point. The draw schedule should be outlined in the contract.

Dual agency. This is when a real estate agent represents both the buyer and seller in a real estate transaction.

Due on sale clause. Nearly every mortgage has a clause that requires the mortgage to be paid off when the home is sold without paying off the mortgage.

Earnest money. When you make an offer, you give the sellers or their agent a deposit to show good faith so they'll take the home off the market for a specified period of time.

Easement. A right given by a landowner to a third party to make use of the land for a specific purpose. Typical easements are for utilities, sewers, water mains, or access to another property. Easements are recorded in the county recorder's office.

Encroachment. A neighbor's fence, driveway, structure, or whatever encroaches on your lot. Many times the property owner doesn't even realize it until a survey is completed.

Equity. The difference between your mortgage balance and the current market value of your home.

Exclusive Agency Listing Agreement. Similar to an Exclusive Right to Sell Listing Agreement except the homesellers can sell to buyers they find through their efforts without paying a commission.

Exclusive Right to Sell Listing Agreement. The listing broker gets the agreed-upon commission regardless of who sells the home.

Fannie Mae. Federal National Mortgage Association.

Freddie Mac. Federal Home Loan Mortgage Corporation.

Ginnie Mae. Government National Mortgage Association.

Good Faith Estimate. Lenders are required to give you in writing a breakdown of all your closing costs and loan fees along with an APR quote within 3 days of your application.

Hazard insurance. Insurance that covers the property against damage and liability.

Home inspection. Usually refers to an inspection performed by a licensed home inspector.

Homeowners association. A corporation formed to handle the affairs of a subdivision, condo, or *PUD* project. All the property owners are members of the association. Officers are elected by the members to enforce the rules, collect fees, and pay the bills.

Home warranty. An insurance policy that insures electrical, plumbing, heating, and appliances in a home for one year. Also, a warranty the builder or a third party issues insuring new construction against defects.

Index. On a *variable rate loan,* it's the base interest rate the lender adds the margin rate to in order to calculate the interest you'll pay for the next period.

Late charge. A penalty applied to a mortgage payment that arrives after the 10- to 15-day grace period. A typical late charge is 4 percent of the payment.

Lead-Based Paint Disclosure. The U.S. Government requires sellers of homes built prior to 1978 to give buyers a filled-out and signed Lead-Based Paint Disclosure form. See www.hud.gov/offices/lead/ disclosurerule/index.cfm.

Lease with option to buy. A lease where the tenant has the right to buy the property for an agreed-upon amount within a certain time period. Sometimes part of the monthly payment is applied to the purchase price if the tenant buys the property as agreed upon.

Leverage. Using mostly borrowed money to buy a property. The buyers have from nothing to only a small percentage of their own money in the deal.

Lien. The legal claim that is recorded and attaches to property.

Lien release. A document that voids the legal rights of the contractor, subcontractors, and suppliers to place a *lien* against your property. You should never close new construction until you have lien releases from all subcontractors and suppliers verifying they have been paid in full for labor and materials.

Limited Agency Consent Agreement. The agent agrees in writing to represent both parties and not disclose anything that would hurt either party's bargaining position.

Listing agreement. A written contract between homesellers and a real estate broker that spells out the terms, commission amount, and time limit of a listing. It's a legally binding agreement, and if you don't understand it, get legal counsel.

Listing exclusion. In an Exclusive Agency Listing Agreement, you exclude certain people who have previously showed interest in your home. The exclusion can be for a certain time period, say 30 days, or it can have no time limit.

Loan commitment. A document that a mortgage provider gives you that states you have been approved for a loan at a certain interest for a certain length of time. It may also have conditions that you need to meet for final approval. A commitment is good for a limited time, usually 30–60 days.

Loan origination fee. A one-time fee charged by the lender to do the loan. It's usually .5 to 1 percent of the loan amount.

Loan-to-value ratio (LTV). The percentage the bank loans you to the value (sales price) of the home. If you borrow 80 percent or put 20 percent down payment, the LTV would be 80 percent. A 10 percent down payment would give you a 90 percent LTV, and so on.

Lock-in. The interest rate the bank offers and you agree to for a certain period of time, usually 30–60 days. Depending on the market, you may lock in a rate at the time of application; other times you may let it float, hoping it will go down before closing.

Maintenance fee. The monthly fee you pay to the *homeowners association* for taking care of the grounds, structures, or whatever else is included in the association agreement.

Mechanic's lien. A *lien* obtained by an unpaid subcontractor or supplier that attaches to your home. Legally, your home can be sold to pay the subcontractor or supplier.

MLS. Realtors' Multiple Listing Service.

Mortgage broker. A person or company that brings together a lender and homebuyer, and processes the mortgage application.

Mortgagee. The entity that lends money secured by property (lender).

Mortgagor. The one who borrows money secured by the property (borrower).

Negative equity. A situation where you owe more on the house than it's worth on the current market.

Nonconforming loan. A loan that doesn't meet with Fannie Mae or Freddie Mac underwriting standards.

Open listing. A written agreement with a real estate broker that if the broker brings in a buyer who buys your home, the broker will receive the commission stated in the listing agreement. It's a non-exclusive, nonmultiple listing service listing. You can give open listings to as many brokers as you want.

Option. A buyer pays a fee to tie up a property for an agreed-on price and length of time. At the end of the time period, the buyer either performs or loses the option fee.

Personal property. Property that is not attached to a dwelling and/or not included in the sale. Examples are refrigerators, furniture, and artwork.

PITI. An acronym for principal, interest, taxes, and insurance when referring to a mortgage payment.

Planned Unit Development (PUD). A community that has a home-owners association that handles common areas. PUDs are typically single-family homes or connected units with a private lot.

Plans and specifications. Drawings for the project, along with a list of the products, materials, quantities, and finishes to be used in the project.

Points. Each point equals 1 percent of the loan amount. Points are usually used to *buy down* an interest rate. What a point is worth can change daily in response to the financial market.

Prepaid interest. Usually interest paid from the day of closing to the end of the month. Your first mortgage payment will then start on the first of the following month. This is so everyone's mortgage payment is due on the first of the month, not a month from the day they close. Also see *points*.

Prepayment penalty. A fee the mortgage company charges you to pay off a loan early. It can be a flat fee or a percentage of the loan amount.

Prequalifying for a loan. A commitment from a bank that you qualify for a loan subject to certain conditions.

Private mortgage insurance (PMI). An insurance premium you pay to protect the bank against default if your loan is more than 80 percent of the purchase price.

PUD. See *Planned Unit Development.*

Punch list. When the home is just about completed, you do a walk-through with the contractor or foreman, and make a list of problems and items to be fixed or completed. Preferably, these items will be completed before you close.

Real estate owned (REO). Homes that lenders have foreclosed on and now own.

Realtor. Someone who is a member of the National Association of Realtors and the appropriate state and local boards.

Regulation Z. Also known as the Truth in Lending Act. It requires lenders to provide a written good faith estimate or a breakdown of the closing costs a buyer pays to get the loan.

Reserve. Money set aside by a condo, co-op, or homeowners association for future improvements and repairs.

RV. Recreational vehicle.

Secondary market. The wholesale mortgage industry.

Seller's disclosure forms. Many states now require sellers to fill out a form that lists the home's components. Typically, sellers will indicate on the form whether each component is working, not working, or explain if a problem exists.

Seller's market. Market conditions that favor the seller, in which there are more homebuyers than homes for sale on the market. The opposite is a *buyer's market*.

Settlement statement. Also known as a *closing statement* or *HUD*. It's a breakdown of all the costs and fees you pay to get a mortgage.

Short sale. Lenders agreeing to take less than the balance owed on a mortgage so that they don't have to foreclose.

Subcontractor. A person or company hired by the contractor to perform specialized work such as framing, sheet-rocking, plumbing, or electrical. Sometimes referred to as a trade contractor.

Title company. A company that insures property against defects in the title. It may also close the loan and prepare closing documents.

Title insurance. An insurance policy that insures your property against problems arising from defects in the title such as *liens*, forgeries, and *easements*.

Town houses. Condominium units that are typically built side by side rather than as multistory units.

Transaction brokerage. A transaction broker working with a consumer without establishing an agency relationship.

Truth in Lending Act. See *Regulation Z*.

Variable interest rate. A mortgage that has an interest rate that goes up or down according to the performance of a financial index. A popular index is the Treasury Bill Index.

Warehousing the loan. Banks and other money sources buying or making mortgage loans for their own portfolios.

Zoning. Local cities' and counties' laws that govern how land is used, and what and where certain structures can be built. These laws are often called zoning ordinances.

Index